TALES OF
VERMONT
WAYS
AND
PEOPLE

TALES OF
VERMONT
WAYS
AND
PEOPLE

BERTHA S. DODGE

Illustrations by Darrell A. Van Citters, Jr.

STACKPOLE BOOKS

TALES OF VERMONT WAYS AND PEOPLE

Copyright © 1977 by
Bertha S. Dodge
Published by
STACKPOLE BOOKS
Cameron and Kelker Streets
P.O. Box 1831
Harrisburg, Pa. 17105

Published simultaneously in Don Mills, Ontario, Canada, by Thomas Nelson & Sons, Ltd.

Printed in the U.S.A.

Library of Congress Cataloging in Publication Data

Dodge, Bertha Sanford, 1902–
    Tales of Vermont ways and people.

    1. Vermont—History. 2. Vermont—Social life and customs. I. Title.
F49.D62   1977   974.3   76-52912
ISBN 0-8117-1722-4

TALES OF VERMONT WAYS AND PEOPLE

Contents

This book attempts to present the birth and growth of a state, not as history with a solemn attention to dates and issues, but through the eyes and minds of people whose families lived during the early hard times and whose lives and character can be measured by the way they faced their trials. Not always accurate as to historical detail—sometimes even demonstrably inaccurate—the accounts they and their children left are, in a way, more accurate than history, for they give a feeling for the kind of people they were and thus the how and why of their state. Today most of these tales are in danger of being forgotten altogether—a loss that future generations would find irreparable.

Perhaps it is no bad thing that the outlines of the ancient Yorker-Vermont feud are fading. Yet a bare fifty years ago there were still living old men whose parents and grandparents had so filled them with tales of the trials of early settlers that they could think of no blacker epithet than "Yorker."

It is this kind of person, living on into the twentieth century, imbued with the old spirit and filled with old tales, who has been responsible for much of what the state has become. Serious history may relegate accounts of the early struggles to a single chapter, but the basic truths embodied in those accounts, whose accuracy of detail historians may question, live on. Hidden away in ancient and sometimes highly partisan accounts, they have needed to be resurrected to give the reader—Vermonter, Yorker, or Any-other-stater—a picture of the past as it looked to past generations.

The contents of this book rely heavily on accounts that are rare and, if in libraries, carefully hoarded. Some few episodes are the result of the writer's personal knowledge, the remainder culled by scanning thousands of pages of fine print on yellowing paper and selecting material that has meaning both to converted Vermonters like herself and to Vermonters of ancient lineage like her husband.

1

The beginnings of Vermont and of her folk tales and legends—
granted it is really possible to assign dates to anything as spon-
taneous as legends—date back to around the year 1760. At that
time, with the French and Indian War ended, settlers began to
spread west from the banks of the Connecticut River toward the
shores of Lake Champlain.

The 1872 historian of the town of Pittsford, situated to the west of
the Green Mountains, wrote:

> Up to 1760, the territory, now the state of Vermont, was
> almost wholly an unbroken wilderness. A few men from
> Massachusetts had located at "Dummer Meadows,"
> within the present limits of Brattleboro; others had built a
> few block-houses and commenced clearings at several
> points further north, on the same side of the Connecticut
> River; and some French Canadians had built temporary
> residences at Chimney Point, in the present town of Ad-
> dison; but till the commencement of the French war a large
> proportion of this region was little known to civilized men,
> few of whom had ever penetrated its sequestered recesses.
>
> This territory had been claimed by the Mohicans . . .
> whose principal seat was at Albany, though they had tem-

porary residences here to which they annually repaired for the purposes of hunting and fishing.

The key word is "temporary." It was the temporary nature of these Indian residences that left the early settlers of Vermont relatively free from the kind of raids that kept pioneers elsewhere in a state of constant alarm. In any case, the first recorded exploration by a white man of the wilderness between the Connecticut River and Lake Champlain is dated 1730. Another diary is dated 1748. In between, and for a dozen years thereafter, many an armed expedition may have passed through that area. What this did, in addition to playing out the "war for conquest—'the game of kings,'" as the historian quoted above put it, was to acquaint the fighters with "the belt of wilderness which mutated into the State of Vermont."

"During the French war," the Pittsford historian wrote, "the New England soldiers engaged in it had a favorable opportunity of becoming acquainted with the country in the vicinity of this and other military routes. Among these soldiers many of the young men were so charmed with the valley of the Otter Creek, that they resolved to make it their future abode. These lands [as were lands all over the future state of Vermont] were claimed by New Hampshire, and had been promised to the soldiers as a reward for their services in conquering the country from the French. But no sooner was peace restored by the conquest of Canada in 1760, than a great crowd of adventurers and speculators made application for them."

New Hampshire Sphere of Influence

Benning Wentworth, then Royal Governor of New Hampshire, had already granted several townships on the west side of the Connecticut River, and thinking this a favorable opportunity for filling his coffers with the fees, continued to make grants, and so rapidly were the surveys extended, that in 1761, no less than sixty townships of six miles square were granted on the west . . . side of the river. Besides the fees and presents this avaricious governor reserved in each township, five hundred acres of land to himself, which was to be free of all taxation . . . In this transaction the claims of the soldiers were entirely disregarded, and the lands passed into the hands of men who sought to enhance their fortunes by selling out their rights to those who wished to become actual settlers.

The charter of Pittsford, the town in which the above historian was interested, was dated October 12, 1762. Of the sixty-four original grantees, none "ever had a permanent residence within its

bounds." However, the first on the list of grantees, Ephraim Doolittle, did concern himself with the township's interests though he finally settled in Shoreham, on the shores of Lake Champlain, where he was a grantee also.

Royal Governor, New Hampshire Style

Before he finally took up residence in Shoreham, Doolittle, shortly to serve as colonel in the Massachusetts Militia during the Revolution, did the future settlers of Pittsford a real service, as described by the town historian:

> As the records of the Proprietors for the first ten years are lost, we have no means of knowing when they organized or who were their first officers; but it is known that at a very early period they proceeded to carry out the provisions of the charter. The township was carefully surveyed, and we are told that Governor Wentworth, in the location of his five hundred acre lot, was made the dupe of a little sharp practice. Capt. Doolittle drew a plan of the township, and in the southeast part it represented a stream of water and the only one on the plan. This he carried to Portsmouth and laid before the Governor, and on being asked what stream was there represented, replied East Creek. His Excellency supposing it to be Otter Creek, and knowing that the lands upon that stream were of the best

quality, said he would have his lot in the southeast corner of the township. It was surveyed off to him and marked B. W. on the plan. Some time after this he had the exquisite pleasure of finding that East Creek was not Otter Creek, but a small stream running through the poorest part of the township.

This might be considered a kind of part payment for the problems Governor Wentworth was busily compounding for the men who paid him for the land, undoubtedly adding something to the official sum for the governor's personal benefit. Such grantees were planning to make more money by selling pieces of their grants to ex-soldiers eager to make permanent homes in the new country. Settlers expected undisputed title to lands they would pay for, clear, plant, and generally improve.

It was soon found that another State asserted its claims to this same territory, and that the validity of their title depended upon contingencies too uncertain to command the confidence of prudent men. A controversy had commenced between New York and New Hampshire respecting their mutual boundary. New York asserted its right to the territory which New Hampshire claimed, and till this was settled, claimants under grants from the latter must remain uncertain whether their claims would prove valid. And it was not until the promulgation of the King's Order in Council of April 11, 1767, which was construed to favor the claims of New Hampshire, that men seeking new homes felt willing to stake their fortunes in this newly granted township.

Such men were soon to be disillusioned and the history of their future state enlivened because of this assumption.

The Duke of York's New World Property

The trouble lay in the pleasant royal custom of rewarding services, past, present, or future, of friends and relatives by granting them huge tracts of land in remote wildernesses. Few such grantees, unless already residing in the colonies, had any idea of removing themselves from the sophisticated delights of London and of the Royal Court. The grants meant money, and the only way to extract money from far away was to sell land to men foolish enough to buy. When settling started, troubles began.

"King Charles the Second," the Pittsford town historian tells us, "on the 12th of March, 1664, issued to his brother James, the Duke of York, a grant of all the land from the west side of the Connecticut River to the east side of Delaware Bay, and the Duke was authorized to employ the necessary force to make his grant available"— "force" meaning whatever measures might be needed to dislodge the Dutch. In September of the same year, the Netherlands relinquished all claim to the land and shortly thereafter commissioners met to settle the question, so fateful to the future state of Vermont, of the boundary line of the Duke of York's grant.

"This decision of the commissioners was accepted for a time . . . but it was soon found that there was a great defect in the language by which the division-line had been defined in 1664, especially in the direction of its northern line, which, running north-northwest, would cross Hudson's river instead of being parallel to its general course." Within less than a century, settlers plagued by insecure titles were demanding that the boundary lines be more clearly defined. Royal governors discussed the matter, royal commissions met over it.

Soon after the establishment of the line between Massachusetts and New Hampshire in 1740, Benning Wentworth of Portsmouth was appointed Governor of the latter province and his commission in defining the limits of his jurisdiction stated that it was to extend westward till it "meets with our other governments" . . . it was generally understood that the eastern boundary of New York was a line beginning at the northwest corner of Connecticut and running at a distance of twenty miles from the Hudson to Lake Champlain . . . The evidence upon this subject was so convincing that Gov. Wentworth did not hesitate to grant townships on the west side of the Connecticut river though careful to avoid encroaching upon the territory of New York. But as this line had not been definitely established, on the 17th November, 1749, the Governor wrote Gov. Clinton that he had it in command from his majesty to make grants of unimproved lands within his government to such persons as would obligate themselves to improve the same; that applications were coming in for the laying out of some townships in the western part of it, and that wishing to avoid, so far as he could, interfering with the government of His Excellency, he enclosed a copy of his commission from the King, and desired to be informed how far north of Albany and how many miles east of Hudson's river, to the northward of the Massachusetts line, his [Gov. Clinton's] government, by his majesty's commission, extended.

This, hinting that the Duke of York's claim stopped twenty miles east of the Hudson, was bound to spark violent controversy. After years of argument, the matter was finally submitted to a Royal Board of Trade (conceivably partial to a royal duke) where "the New York claim was urged with so much skill and vehemence, that in July, 1764, an order was obtained from the King in council, declaring 'the west bank of the Connecticut . . . to be the boundary-line between the two provinces of New Hampshire and New York.' The territory thus annexed to New York comprised the whole of the State of Vermont, and having up to this time been considered a part of New Hampshire, a large proportion of it had been granted in townships of six miles square by Gov. Wentworth and in a few of these were quite flourishing settlements."

These New Hampshire grantees, not consulted in the matter, of course, might have accepted the jurisdiction of New York, "but when the New York government went farther, and, disregarding the claims of the settlers, proceeded to grant their property to other parties, it aroused the most serious indignation." Concerned settlers of Pittsford sent a plea to the government of New York stating that "great scruples arose in our minds with regard to the validity of our aforesaid grant . . . & being desirous of obtaining a confirmation of our Grants and of becoming inhabitants in said Government of New York . . . we pray that your Honour will receive this our humble adress, and while we are pursuing our settlements, bear in mind our sinsear endeavours to become a respectable part of your Honour's government."

Royal Governors of New York

Concerned more with possible profits than with respectable, hardworking settlers, the New York governor ignored the touching plea from Pittsford and "finding this a favorable opportunity for enhancing his private fortune by the fees, carried on a lucrative business in the granting of townships, till his career was suddenly arrested by the notorious Stamp Act of the British Parliament, which required all instruments of contract . . . to be executed upon stamped paper, for which a duty was to be paid to the Crown; and any contract not thus executed was to be null and void." Furious colonists everywhere were confiscating those stamps "so that none found their way into places of business. As all land patents were to be void unless stamped, and as the stamps could not be obtained, further grants by the New York governor had to be temporarily suspended."

New York governors had other ways to fill their pockets at the settlers' expense. The new governor who arrived the following year made a feeble gesture at conciliation by assuring the settlers they might receive confirmation of their claims. All they had to do was to pay to New York fees set by that colony. This, as it turned out, "virtually amounted to a prohibition. The fees to the governor of New Hampshire for the granting of a township, were about one hundred dollars, while under the government of New York, two thousand or two thousand six hundred were demanded for a confirmation of one of the charters. This unreasonable demand could hardly be complied with, inasmuch as most of the early settlers were men of slender means who had expended what they had, in acquiring the New Hampshire title to their lands and in making improvements thereon."

The settlers, finding their petition totally ignored, sent a representative to England in 1767 to lay the matter directly "before His Majesty." This man returned with a document which stated, among other things, that "the power of granting lands was vested in the governors of the colony, originally, for the purpose of accommodating, not distressing settlers, especially the poor and industrious.

"The unreasonableness of obliging a very large tract of country to pay a *second time* the immense sum of £33,000 in fees, according to the allegations of this petition, for no other reason than its being found necessary to settle the line of boundary between the colonies, is so unjustifiable that His Majesty is not only determined to have the strictest inquiry made into the circumstances of the charge, but expects the clearest and fullest answer to every part of it."

There were unfortunately no teeth in this high-sounding document. The New York governor who, after a single year in power, retired in 1770, had, despite the royal interdictions, granted patents in the disputed area that "covered more than six hundred thousand acres of government lands, and he had realized from the same about $25,000 in money beside reserving to himself, in the name of others, more than twenty thousand acres."

This governor's successor was Earl Dunmore, "a rapacious Scottish peer" who "as proof of his industry . . . in the short space of eight months granted to speculators four hundred and fifty thousand acres of Vermont lands and received fees for the same, and also had granted to himself in the name of others fifty-one thousand acres more." Ironically, Vermont's lovely Lake Dunmore is this man's enduring if undeserved monument.

The account runs thus: "Lord Dunmore and his party came up the Leicester River to the site of Salisbury village, and from thence on foot over to the lake [3 to 4 miles] where the Earl waded into the water a few steps, and pouring upon the waves a libation of wine, proclaimed, 'Ever after, this body of water shall be called Lake Dunmore, in honor of the Earl of Dunmore.' Two Indians bend down and split the branches of a small tree standing near, insert the emptied bottle, and the christening ceremony is finished."

2

The Green Mountain Boys

In Albany rapacious New York governor succeeded rapacious New York governor. In the disputed lands, settlers of New Hampshire grants who had cleared land and put up homes found themselves harassed by men who claimed the land under New York grants. A test case was brought into court in Albany, where the lieutenant governor, the prosecuting attorney, and the presiding judge turned out to be interested parties. Inevitably the New York grants won out and sheriffs were directed to "execute the writs in the ejectment suits."

Psychological Warfare, Eighteenth-Century Style

The times demanded a Robin Hood and his band and soon found one. When the ejecting sheriff arrived, he was faced by "the settlers assembled in arms and they 'threatened,' as he said, 'to blow his brains out.'" Returning to Albany, the sheriff gathered a force of over three hundred men "of all grades and professions." The forewarned settlers "had made the necessary preparation for effectual resistance." Thereupon, valuing their lives more than the contested lands, the posse withdrew and left the New Hampshire grantees in undisputed possession of the field.

Though, for appearance's sake, the New York governor was making grants in tracts of no more than a thousand acres each, the grantees were soon conveying their grants to speculators—one James Duane, a New York attorney, accumulating title to some fifteen thousand acres. To clinch his possession, he soon was sending out a surveyor named William Cockburn, who wrote Duane a letter describing his reception by residents near Otter Creek.

> I have run out lots from the south bounds to within about two miles of the Great Falls. I found it vain to persist any longer, as they were resolved at all events to stop us; there have been many threats pronounced against me. Gideon Cooley, who lives by the Great Falls, headed the party who was to shoot me . . . and your acquaintance Nathaniel Allen, was in the woods with another, blacked and dressed like Indians as I was informed . . . The inhabitants denied that they *knowed* any thing about these men, though the people of Durham assured me that these men pretended to murder us if we did not go from thence, and advised me by all means to desist from running through . . . On my assuring them that I would survey no more in those parts, we were permitted to proceed along the Crown Point road with the hearty prayers of the women as we passed never to return.

When, by virtue of the psychological warfare described in the above letter, New York patentees found themselves unable to collect the expected fees, they "proceeded to dispose of these lands to other New York parties, who, in attempting to locate them, met with no very encouraging success."

A Benjamin Spencer, whom James Duane had hired to collect fees in "Socialborough," the New York grantors' name for Pittsford, reported in a letter:

> The people of Socialborough decline buying their lands, saving four or five [these undoubtedly New York grantees] and say they will defend them by force. The New Hampshire people strictly forbid any farther survey being made in Socialborough, or any settlements being made only [except] under the New Hampshire title . . . You may ask why I do not proceed against them in a due course of law, but you need not wonder when I tell you that it has got to that the people go armed and guards set in the roads to examine people what their business is, and where they are going and if they do not give a particular account, they are beaten in a most shamefull manner, and it has got to that they say they will not be brought to justice by this

province, and bid defiance to any authority in the province . . . I hope the survey of our patent may not be stopped on account of this tumult, as we shall labor under a great disadvantage if our lands are not divided this spring. I look upon it to be dangerous for Mr. Cockburn to come into the country until these people can be subdued . . . I desire that some person may be employed hereabout that we may know where our land is, which I should be glad you would inform me of as soon as possible . . . One Ethan Allen hath brought from Connecticut twelve or fifteen of the most blackguard fellows he can get, double armed in order to protect him, and if some method is not taken to subdue the towns of Bennington, Shaftsbury, Arlington, Manchester and those people in Socialborough, and others scattered about the woods, there had as good be an end of government.

Robin Hood and his band had stepped upon the scene. The "Bennington Mob" or, as Lieutenant Governor Colden of New York was pleased to call them, "that set of lawless people," was taking over.

The Bennington Mob

The writer of the above letter, Benjamin Spencer, settled under a New York title in Clarendon, somewhat to the south of Rutland, was a dyed-in-the-wool Tory who, in 1777, would seek the protection of Burgoyne at Ticonderoga. His 1773 harassment by Ethan Allen and his Green Mountain Boys is described in a deposition made by a sympathetic fellow Yorker:

> That about eleven o'clock night on Saturday the 20th instant, as the deponent is informed and verily believes, Remember Baker, Ethan Allen, Robert Cochrane and a number of other persons, armed with guns, cutlasses &c., came to the house of Benjamin Spencer, Esq. of said Durham who holds his farm under a title derived from the government of New York, and break open the said house, and took the said Spencer and carried him about two miles to the house of Thomas Green of Kelso, and there kept him in custody until Monday morning. The heads of the said rioters then asked the said Spencer whether he would choose to be tried at the house of Joseph Smith in said Durham, or at his the said Spencer's own door. To which Spencer replied that he was guilty of no crime, but if he must be tried, he would choose to have his trial at his own

door and proceeded to his trial before Seth Warner of Bennington; the said Remember Baker, Ethan Allen and Robert Cochrane who sat as judges. That said rioters charged the said Spencer with being a great friend to the government of New York and had acted as a magistrate of the county of Charlotte; of which respective charges his said judges found him guilty, and passed sentence that said Spencer's house should be burned to the ground.

Ethan Allen called it "a burnt offering to the gods of the woods."

In addition, Spencer was to agree not to act again as magistrate for New York.

Spencer thereupon urged that his wife and children would be ruined, and his store of dry goods and all his property wholly destroyed, if his house was burned. Warner then declared that Spencer's house should not be wholly destroyed, that only the roof should be taken off and put on again, provided Spencer would declare that it was put on under New Hampshire title and purchase a right under the charter from the last mentioned government. These several conditions Spencer was obliged to comply with, upon which the rioters dismissed him.

Spencer, of course, was known in the vicinity. Had he been a stranger trying to make New York surveys, he might have been given the "Beech-seal"—flogged with a beech twig—then forced to promise never again to serve the province of New York among New Hampshire grants. Then, feeling their prisoner had been sufficiently punished, they would give him a certificate stating that the offender had had his trial and "this is his discharge from us," which should "be sufficient permit or pass among the New Hampshire claimants or Green Mountain Boys"—this latter name being assumed in derision for New York Governor Tryon's statement that he expected to drive the band into the Green Mountains.

One such pass, dated "Nov. 26, A.D. 1773," in Arlington, ran: "These may Sertify that Jacob Marsh hath been examined, had a fair trial. So that our mob shall not meddle further with him as long as he behaves. Sartified by his Judges, to wit: Samuel Tubs, Nathaniel Spencer, Philip Perry. Teste, Lt. Seth Warner."

"Green Mountain Boys," the Pittsford town historian wrote, "soon became an honorable appellation, and is associated with some of the most brilliant military achievements in the early history of our country." Conversely, the appellation "Yorker" became, to the men of the Green Mountains, highly derogatory. Even into the twentieth century, old-timers who in their youth must have known other old-timers to whom the status of the New Hampshire grants was not quite a dead issue were inclined to reject out of hand any movement that had its inception among the Yorkers of their and our century.

Questions have been raised by historians of our day not only as to whose interests the Green Mountain Boys and their boisterous methods were serving, but also as to whose interests some of them—notably the Allens—really wished to serve. Of course, there is no clear answer. Motives are never altogether simple and it may well be that the Allens, who themselves later became land speculators, were keeping their own interests in mind.

The motivation belongs to the rough times in which the Green Mountain Boys lived. What belongs to our times and all times is the body of legends such picturesque characters generated. Swaggering in a wildly original uniform of his own design, telling tall stories of his exploits and promising taller yet to come, Ethan Allen is a figure time enhances, while the proper, unimaginative royal governors fade into the background.

The Allens

Today we still delight in the legendary exploits of the Allen brothers and cousins—Ethan, Ira, Levi, Zimri, Heber, Heman, and others—plus their comrades, among whom were Seth Warner and that man of the memorable name, Remember Baker (both also Allen cousins). Nevertheless, we might also spare a moment's sympathy for the harassed New York governors. Had their emissaries been slaughtered or even seriously hurt, they could have sent in regular troops to chastise the irritating rebels. How does a governor deal with an episode like the following? Acknowledge it and he makes himself and his fellow Yorkers ridiculous. Ignore it and he asks for more of the same.

Ethan Allen's Little Joke

Two New York sheriffs—representatives, of course, of the New York governors—were caught by Ethan Allen on disputed lands and duly locked up separately for the night. Then, during the hours of darkness, Ethan hung a dummy in a distant tree which could be seen from both of the rooms in which the sheriffs had been lodged. By the dawn's early light Ethan awakened each of his guests in turn, let each view, as by chance, the dangling figure, and allowed to each that it might be the figure of his fellow sheriff. Then, carelessly forgetting to lock the door, he let his horrified prisoners escape separately. Only when the two met in Albany did they realize they had been the victims of one of Ethan Allen's grim little jokes.

Superb master of psychological warfare that he was, Ethan was all too conscious that the New Hampshire grantees needed something to laugh about and that the laugh would be most enjoyed when a New York sheriff was made the butt of such a hoax. Yet, for all his boisterous pranks, he was no illiterate yokel but a man of real worth of whom George Washington would say, "There is an original something in him that commands admiration."

Seizure of Fort Ticonderoga

In the spring of 1779, Ethan Allen, by then a colonel in the Continental Army, had been a British prisoner of war for two and a half years. He wrote and had published the narrative of events that led up to that captivity:

> . . . the first systematical and bloody attempts at Lexington, to enslave America, thoroughly electrified my mind, and fully determined me to take part with my country: And while I was wishing for an opportunity to signalize myself in its behalf, directions were privately sent to me from the then colony (now state) of Connecticut, to raise the Green Mountain Boys; (and if possible) with them surprise and take the fortress Ticonderoga.

For the Green Mountain Boys to seize a fortress on New York territory must have been an assignment after his and their hearts.

This enterprise I cheerfully undertook; and after guarding all the several passes that led thither, to cut off all intelligence between the garrison and the country, made a forced march from Bennington, and arrived at the lake opposite to Ticonderoga [over 100 miles from Bennington] on the evening of the ninth day of May, 1775, with two hundred and thirty valiant Green Mountain Boys; and it was with the utmost difficulty that I procured boats to cross the lake: However I landed eighty-three men near the garrison, and sent boats back to the rear guard commanded by col. Seth Warner; but the day began to dawn, and I found myself under a necessity to attack the fort, before the rear could cross the lake; and, as it was viewed hazardous, I harangued the officers and soldiers in the manner following;

"Friends and fellow soldiers, you have for a number of years past, been a scourge and terror to arbitrary power. Your valour has been famed abroad, and acknowledged, as appears by the advice and orders to me (from the general assembly of Connecticut) to surprise and take the garrison now before us. I now propose to advance before you, and in person conduct you through the wicket gate, for we must this morning either quit our pretensions to valour, or possess ourselves of this fortress in a few minutes; and, in as much as it is a desperate attempt, (which none but the bravest men dare undertake) I do not urge it on any contrary to his will. You that will undertake voluntarily, poise your firelocks."

The men being (at this time) drawn up in three ranks, each poised his firelock . . . and, at the head of the centre file I marched them immediately to the wicket-gate aforesaid, where I found a centry posted, who instantly snapped his fusee at me; I ran immediately toward him, and he retreated through the covered way into the parade within the garrison, gave a halloo and ran under a bomb-proof . . . The garrison being asleep (except the centries) we gave three huzzas which greatly surprised them. One of the centries made a pass at one of my officers with a charged bayonet and slightly wounded him: My first thought was to kill him with my sword; but, in an instant, altered the design and fury of the blow to a slight cut on the side of the head; upon which he dropped his gun, and asked quarter, which I readily granted him, and demanded of him the place where the commanding officer kept; he shewed me a pair of stairs in the front of a barrack, to which I immediately repaired, and ordered the commander (capt. Delaplace) to come forth instantly, or I would sacrifice the whole garrison; at which the capt. came immediately to the door with his breeches in his hand, when I ordered him to deliver to me the fort instantly, who asked me by what authority I demanded it; I answered, "In the name of the great Jehovah, and the Continental Congress." (The authority of the Congress being very little known at that time) he began to speak again; but I interrupted him, and with my drawn sword over his head, again demanded an immediate surrender of the garrison.

Picture if you can the sleep-befuddled British officer, breeches in hand, peering through the gray light of dawn at the weirdly uniformed apparition that represented at one and the same time the awful majesty of the great Jehovah and the mysterious power of a strange entity called the Continental Congress! Truly a man from Mars against whom resistance must be futile! The officer "complied and ordered his men to be forthwith paraded without arms."

This surprise [Ethan Allen continued] was carried into execution in the gray of the morning on the 10th day of

May, 1775. The sun seemed to rise that morning with a superior lustre; and Ticonderoga and its dependencies smiled on its conquerors, who tossed about the flowing bowl, and wished success to Congress, and the liberty and freedom of America. Happy it was for me (at that time) that the then future pages of the book of fate, which afterwards unfolded a miserable scene of two years and eight months imprisonment, was hid from my view.

Ethan Allen's capture would take place in September, 1775, during an ill-fated attack on Montreal. But four months earlier the flowing bowl was being happily filled from Captain Delaplace's store, for ninety gallons of which Ethan Allen duly wrote a receipt. It was, however, the capture of the solid military stores that was the raid's chief objective and constituted its real success.

The Tory Allen

The large Allen family encompassed men of all kinds, from the active Green Mountain Boys, Ethan and Ira and some less famous brothers, to the admitted Tory, Levi, to whom the British would later be paying a pension of 100 pounds a year. Levi, as ruggedly individualistic in his own way as the others and smarting under the loss of his lands by confiscation (a fate suffered by all land-owning Tories), is supposed to have composed the following verses about himself and Whig brothers Ira and Ethan. Ethan was also a deist, a person who, while accepting a personal God, rejected the then current ideas on Christian revelation—a way of thought unacceptable to the ordained ministers of his day.

THE THREE BROTHERS

Old Ethan once said o'er a full bowl of grog,
Though I believe not in Jesus, I hold to a God;
There is also a Devil—you will see him some day
In a whirlwind of fire take Levi away.

Says Ira to Ethan, it plain doth appear
That you are inclined to banter and jeer;
I think for myself and freely declare
Our Levi's too stout for the prince of the air;
If ever you see them engaged in affray,
'Tis our Levi who'll take the Devil away.

Says Levi, your speech makes it perfectly clear
That you both are inclined to banter and jeer;
Though through all the world my name stands enrolled
For tricks sly and crafty, ingenious and bold,

> There is one consolation which none can deny,
> That there's one greater rogue in this world than I.
>
> "Who's that?" they both cry with equal surprise.
> "'Tis Ira! 'Tis Ira! I give him the prize."

Captain Benjamin Marvin of Grand Isle told of an encounter with Levi Allen while he was at court in Burlington. Levi came into the boarding house somewhat late, "the court, bar, and other boarders being seated at the table. Stepping up to the table, he remarked that he had conscientious scruples in regard to eating without asking the Divine blessing. Spreading forth his hands, they all arose.

"'O God!' said he, 'forgive us our sins and may the world forgive us our debts; and then what little we have left will be our own; and may God Almighty damn the attorneys to hell. Amen.'"

Ann Story

Not a member of the Green Mountain Boys, but deserving to be enrolled among them, was widow Ann Story, who lived in a cabin near the banks of Otter Creek. When at about the time Ticonderoga was taken, she discovered Yorkers nearby, she tore a blank leaf from her Bible and, so legend has it, sent it by a friendly Indian to the leader of the Green Mountain Boys with the words, "The Philistines be upon thee, Sampson!" thus demonstrating both her literacy and where her sympathies lay.

In September, 1774, Amos Story, with his oldest son, Solomon, had come to his Salisbury grant, put up a small log house, and commenced clearing his land

> with the expectation of raising wheat sufficient to supply bread to his family, which he intended to move into the new home the following year.
>
> But a few weeks after he had commenced his clearing he was killed by the fall of a tree. Solomon, who at that time was a lad about fourteen years old, was at work with his father in the woods at the time of the accident, and was compelled to chop the tree quite off in two places (and it was a large sugar maple) before he could roll it off his father, who was already dead underneath it. . . .
>
> Soon after the death of Amos Story, Solomon returned to his friends in Rutland, and carried the sad intelligence of his father's death to his bereaved mother, and other relatives.

Ann Story had been waiting with her younger children with Rutland friends until the Salisbury home might be ready. A lesser woman would have given up the idea of going on to the wilderness that was then Salisbury. Not so Mrs. Story.

> Mrs. Story was a woman of very large stature and masculine appearance, and possessed all that physical strength and hardihood which her looks would indicate. Few men ever possessed so much resolution, firmness and fearlessness as she. Possessed of good health and an iron constitution, she feared neither tory, Indian, or wild beast.
>
> She could use the axe with a skill and power which few of her neighbors, though most of them were stalwart men, could equal; and in handling the lever, in rolling logs, every one admitted her to be among the foremost and most efficient.
>
> Having such qualifications as these, Mrs. Story—in company with her three boys, Solomon, Ephraim, and Samuel, and her two daughters, Hannah and Susanna—moved to their farm in Salisbury in the latter part of the year 1775, and took possession of the log house her husband and son had erected for their reception the year previous . . .
>
> Here she labored with her boys on the farm, taking the lead in the labors of clearing the land, raising grain and other products necessary to sustain her growing family, until the early part of the year 1777.

As war clouds thickened, neighbors began to leave their grants because of dread of the Indians, whom the enemy might be egging on as had the French two decades earlier. Ann Story compromised by taking her family to spend the winters near Rutland, always returning to Salisbury in the spring. A neighbor wrote of her:

> Mrs. Story was a woman of profound integrity. What she said might always be relied upon as truth. The writer lived a neighbor to her from his infancy to the time of her death, and can vouch for the scrupulousness she always manifested for the truth of her stories (of which she used to tell a great many), concerning the times of the American Revolution . . .
>
> She was a true whig of the times of the revolution, and participated greatly in the spirit of her party; and her position in this new country gave her opportunities to show that she was not a friend to the government of the United States in name only, but was ready to make sacrifices for it. Indeed, her house was an asylum for all her country's friends. She worked zealously against the royalists, and earned for herself quite an illustrious name as a heroine.

The following incident took place early in the spring of 1776, after most of the settlers had left the country, and is given nearly in her own words:

"The snow had melted away from the mountains, and the creek had become so swollen as to overflow all the low lands in its vicinity, when a party of Indians came from the north, seeking booty, pillaging all the houses they could find, and afterward burning them, together with barns, farming tools, and other things of value. The first intimation we had of the presence of these Indians, was the discovery of them pillaging Mr. Graves' house, which stood about seventy rods from ours.

"As Mr. Graves left his farm in September of the year previous, and had not returned, the Indians probably found nothing of value, so they set fire to his house and came over to ours, not, however, until we had secured our most valuable articles of household goods, and safely deposited them in our canoe, which lay at the water's edge [Otter Creek], but a few steps from our door. Unobserved by the Indians, we shoved off our boat, and were soon fairly out of their reach in the deep water of the swamp. Even if the Indians did see us they were unable to follow, as they had no canoes, having left them in Canada or at Lake Champlain, not expecting to need them on this inland excursion.

"We stationed ourselves back in the swamp, at a considerable distance from the house, where we could observe their movements and make sure the hour and direction of their departure. Here we saw Mr. Graves' house and our own burn down at the hand of our cruel foes. When the houses were burnt so nearly down that there was no longer hope of saving them, the Indians departed to the north, and we retraced our course, and soon landed in safety all our moveable treasure. The spot on which so recently stood our rude but comfortable house was now made desolate; but our spirits were not crushed. If the smoking ruins of our dwelling suggested too plainly the dangers of our situation and disheartened us, the hope arose that, as the Indians had made so little in this excursion, they might not visit this region for booty any more. So we immediately made arrangements for building a new house, and by cutting and laying up small trees, such as we could handle without a team, it was not long before we had quite a comfortable dwelling, made of poles instead of logs, on the spot where the former one had stood . . ."

The fact that most of the early settlers had at this time left the country, some to fight the battles of the Revolution, and others for the better security of their persons and property, rendered the condition of those who remained on their lands extremely hazardous, particularly on account of the hostility of the Indians; but Mrs. Story could not be induced to leave. By her persevering and indomitable spirit she appeared determined to overcome every obstacle which might prevent her from clearing and cultivating her farm. And, in order to render herself and family more secure from the attacks of the enemy, especially in the night, she hit upon the following expedient:

"We dug a cavern in the bank of the creek, where we could retire for the night, cooking and taking our meals at the house, and laboring on the farm in the day time. The cavern or cave we made by digging horizontally into the bank of the creek, concealing the dirt we removed, under the water. The passage at the mouth of the cave was sufficient only to admit our canoe so that all must lie prostrate in passing either in or out. This passage was dug so low and so deep that the canoe could float into the cave quite out of sight. The place where we slept was higher ground, and was an excavation by the side of and above the passageway from the canoe, and of sufficient size to accommodate the whole family. We took the precaution to cut and stick down bushes at the mouth of the cave, both when we were in and out of it, so that the place of entrance would appear like the rest of the bank, and thus, prevent discovery. The fact that the banks of Otter Creek were sought at this time by the traveler and adventurer as a more safe guide than marked trees or uncertain footpaths, rendered this precaution the more necessary."

Mrs. Story used to relate an incident connected with this subterraneous retreat, which seems to be of some importance, as it corroborates the truth of other facts in connection with this remarkable women. It was as follows:

A woman by the name of _____ had been made captive by the Indians, but was so far advanced in pregnancy that she was unable to keep up with her captors on their journey, and so, loitering behind, was at last left to find her way back to her friends the best way she could. This woman found an asylum at the house of Mrs. Story, and by her was protected and cared for during her confinement.

The time, place, or circumstances of the birth of the child cannot be related at this late day; but it is certain that the child was born, and gave Mrs. Story's family great anxiety and trouble, on account of its crying when they were in the cave, as this might lead to the discovery of their nightly abode. In fact, their fears were shortly realized, under the following circumstances.

Very early one morning, before the inmates of the cave had taken their departure, Ezekiel Jenny, well known to Mrs. Story as a tory, was passing by on foot, on the bank of the creek, when his attention was arrested by the crying of the child. At this unexpected sound he stopped and listened, and finally waited until Mrs. Story pushed her canoe, with its precious freight, into the creek, from its retreat hitherto so obscure and safe.

When the party in the canoe landed at their usual place, sixty or seventy rods below, Jenny interrogated Mrs. Story concerning some of the movements of the whigs, to whom she gave evasive and dissatisfactory answers. This exasperated Jenny "and," to use her own language, "he threatened to shoot me upon the spot; but to all this I bid defiance, and told him I had no fears of being shot by so consummate a coward as he; and finally he passed along down the creek, and I lost no time in notifying Foot and Bentley that tories were within our borders; and immediately all the whigs who could be raised were set upon their track, and overtook them the same day in Monkton, and that night captured every one of them, to the number of about twenty, and delivered them up to our authorities at Ticonderoga."

A Green Mountain Boy in spirit, if not in fact, Ann Story reached her cabin one day to find the door barred from the inside. The arrival of the Yorkers soon afterwards convinced her that whoever was hiding inside the cabin could not be one of them. She received the Yorkers quietly and when they asked who was inside the barred door, she told them that she always kept the cabin barred so that neither she nor her children would be troubled by wild animals or Indians. If they—the Yorkers—wished to enter, they might enter as she did: by climbing to the roof, lifting a square of the bark that served for roofing, and dropping inside. They declined the offer and took their departure, whereupon she, knowing the Yorkers might be watching her actions, climbed to the roof and entered to find, as she expected, a contingent of the Green Mountain Boys inside.

Judge Painter

Gamaliel Painter, eventually to become the judge whose name survives in Painter Hall of Middlebury College, was an admirer and associate of Ethan Allen, whom he had known as a young man before he left Connecticut for Vermont. He was "intimately associated with him, Warner, and Baker in their movements." It was this association, undoubtedly, that led him, when in his early thirties, to make a risky visit to

> the British post at Crown Point in order to spy out the enemy's conditions and plans. He played the part of a half idiot, taking with him a basket in which he carried a little butter, a few eggs, and some notions to sell among the soldiers . . . The guard had been instructed to let no suspicious looking person pass and Painter, notwithstanding his appropriate dress and foolish appearance, looked somewhat suspicious.
>
> Instead of being admitted to the fort, he was rowed towards a large boat where superior officers were to examine him. He knew he was in the power of an enemy who would soon be able to prove the falsity of his feigned character. He saw the eyes of the officers near the rowboat were watching his every movement; but, as though seeing not, suspecting not, and casting himself down into the boat, he began to count over to himself the profits of his traffic. If he sold mother's butter for so much per pound and sister Suzy's eggs for so much apiece . . . this innocent unconcern and idiotic gibbering saved him. The officers began to dread the ridicule it might bring upon them to take so much pains to capture a perfect idiot, and upon a little consultation, turned their boat about and allowed him to enter the fort and traffic with the soldiers, which being done, he hurried his departure with a fixed resolution never to hazard his life in another such undertaking.

Of course, though, he did not escape more such hazards. "At another time, passing through a Tory nest in Clarendon, meeting three men on horseback, he escaped suspicion by boldly inquiring, before they could challenge him" the way to the residence of their leader, where he knew the Tories must rendezvous.

Ethan Allen's Tory Neighbor

If a man knew how to behave, being a Loyalist and Tory in spirit did not necessarily expose a settler to attack by Whig neighbors. In Arlington, the Canfield family (of which the late enthusiastic Vermont author, Dorothy Canfield Fisher, has been one of this century's members) maintained the respect of even the rambunctious Allens while never denying their Loyalist sympathies. Nathan Canfield,

Esq., who moved to Arlington about 1768, "seemed to have a habit of assisting the needy" without inquiring into their political opinions. Whoever came to his door hungry was fed, and if needing shelter, he received it. "No needy person ever left his house unrelieved . . . Being a man of great sagacity and prudence, he retained in a great degree the confidence of both parties. His connections and his sympathies were probably in favor of the loyalists, yet to the end he enjoyed the friendship of Allen, Warner, Baker and the other leaders. On one occasion, when a man from Sunderland raised his gun to shoot him, Colonel Allen rushed between them for his protection. He was sometimes arrested and fined but succeeded in preserving himself from material harm."

The Lyon of Vermont

Quite as memorable as the Allens, though less remembered today, is the hulking, swashbuckling Irishman, Matthew Lyon. Orphaned in Ireland when barely past his fourteenth birthday and seeing no future for himself in his native land, he sought out a sea captain in 1765 and persuaded the man to take the gamble of giving him passage to America. It was not then unusual for ocean passage to be paid for after arrival at an American port by auctioning off the passenger's services for a sum which he must then work out.

Lyon's purchaser was a merchant from Litchfield, Connecticut, in whose vicinity lived the Allen brothers together with their miscellaneous cousins. Their Whig sentiments were altogether to Matthew Lyon's taste. Soon finding his employer a convinced Tory, Matthew decided to free himself from his indenture as soon as he could find a way to do so. When, in a neighboring town, he saw a team of two-year-old bulls he knew his employer would covet, he persuaded the bulls' owner to let him have them on a promise that they should be fully paid for once his apprenticeship was completed. Persuasive and appealing, young Lyon took the bulls to Litchfield and used them to buy off his apprenticeship. Ever after, Matthew Lyon's favorite oath was, "By the bulls that redeemed me!"

Soon Lyon was working in the Allen Iron Works in Salisbury, Connecticut, and by 1771 was binding his fortunes still more closely to the Allen family by marrying Ethan's niece. Three years later the young couple was starting north with their two children, in the company of Thomas Chittenden and family. The older Chittenden would eventually serve as governor of the then not yet existent state, Vermont. The two families settled a bit to the north of Bennington, where Lyon would presently join the Green Mountain Boys and Chittenden, if not actually serving with them, became one of their loyal supporters.

Forty years later Matthew Lyon would draw a word picture of the doings of that band:

> In 1774, when British encroachment on our rights was raising the spirit of resistance, I laid before the youngerly men in my neighborhood, in the country now called Vermont, a plan for armed association which was adopted . . . With a part of this company of Minute Men, immediately after the battle of Lexington, I joined Ethan Allen. Eighty-five of us took from one hundred and forty British veterans the fort Ticonderoga, which contained artillery and warlike stores which drove the British from Boston and aided in taking Burgoyne and Cornwallis. That fort contained when we took it more cannon, mortarpieces and other military stores than could be found in all the revolted colonies.

In addition to gaining those valuable military stores, the eloquent Irishman "persuaded many of the Royal Irish Company taken there to join us, who afterwards distinguished themselves in our cause."

In 1793, Matthew Lyon settled in today's Fair Haven, where he started several industries, among them a sawmill and an iron foundry which used scrap iron collected on various Revolutionary battlefields—literally turning into ploughshares and pruning hooks the weapons of war. He also established a brick kiln which produced bricks such as went into his fine old house that long faced the Fair Haven town square.

Most important for the future, the man who as a lad in Ireland had served as a printer's devil, purchased a printing press and, from shot picked up on battlefields, cast the type he needed. For paper, then almost exclusively made from rags, he experimented with wood pulp and finally produced from basswood pulp paper for his newspaper, first named *Farmer's Library,* then *Fair Haven Gazette.* The year 1798 saw him publishing a bimonthly magazine with the resounding title, *The Scourge of the Aristocracy and Repository of Important Political Truth.*

A Scotchman who visited New England about then wrote of the town: "Fair Haven joins on Skenesborough [now Whitehall, New York] and is the most flourishing town in the State. It owes its consequence to its founder, Colonel Lyon . . . He has held some of the first offices in the State . . . His friendship and generosity are as great as his ambition."

Lyon represented Fair Haven in the General Assembly of Vermont (1794-1795) and by 1796 was moving on to the United States Congress, where he soon made himself conspicuous as a "democrat" who regarded Federalists as thinly disguised Tories. His biographer wrote:

Between Lyon and the Tories or Federalists there was implacable hostility. At him they hurled shafts of ridicule and opprobrium; at them he levelled barbed arrows of denunciation and scornfully fierce invective of a nature suggested by the quotation (from Defoe) he printed on the front page of his Lyon Magazine:

> Nature has left this Tincture in the Blood,
> That all men would be Tyrants if they cou'd—
> If they forbear their Neighbors to devour,
> 'Tis not from want of Will but want of Power.

It was foreordained that when, in May, 1797, Matthew Lyon took his place in the Congress, he would soon be roaring defiance at President John Adams, whom he considered a confirmed Tory.

The president's partisans tried, by vote, to have Lyon expelled from Congress. Failing in this, recourse was had to the newly passed "Alien and Sedition Laws." These laws, passed at President Adams' request and limited to his term of office, authorized the president to order out of the United States such alien-born persons as the president might judge to be a threat to the peace and safety of the country. Furthermore, any person printing or publishing any malicious writing against the government or president could be subjected to heavy fines and imprisonment. Since the Constitution expressly states that "Congress shall make no law abridging the freedom of speech, or of the press," Colonel Lyon, suspecting himself to be the main target of the new law, was soon roaring defiance.

Unfortunately, twenty-four days earlier he had sent a letter to the *Vermont Journal* of Windsor, Vermont, answering an attack on himself by a Federalist enemy. The Federalist editor of that paper held the letter for over three weeks until the new law was enacted and then published it. Matthew Lyon was duly indicted, it being the first and one of the few indictments ever returned under the notorious law.

With a federal jury selected from among the Federalist sympathizers in the state spurred on by the realization that an unfriendly vote in Congress could change the teetering balance of power, Lyon was found guilty, sentenced to four months' imprisonment, and ordered to pay a considerable fine. This, of course, focused popular attention on the man the Federalists hated, so that when a new election was held during his imprisonment, Lyon won by a larger than ever margin.

Matthew Lyon expected that as soon as he was released from the Vergennes jail a new federal indictment and a new fine would be awaiting him. It was a bitter cold morning in February, 1799, when, his release being expected, a long line of sleighs drew up beside the jail on the ice of Otter Creek. Lyon was touched to realize that the Green Mountain Boys were gathered there in force. As thousands more Vermonters gathered there, old Senator Mason from Virginia rode up, dismounted, hitched his horse to a tree, and, after introducing himself to the assembled crowd, announced that he had ridden all the way from Virginia to make certain, for himself and his friends—Thomas Jefferson, James Madison, James Monroe, and others—that Matthew Lyon would not be thrust back into jail for lack of the needed fine. In his saddlebags he had the sum—$1060.96— in gold so that there need be no question of legal tender.

Meanwhile Lyon's old friend, Apollos Austin of Orwell, appeared with the amount of the fine in silver dollars. The Green Mountain Boys had other ideas. One of them mounted a stump to declare that he and his fellows intended to liberate their former member. Each would lay on the stump whatever he could spare—a quarter or half-dollar perhaps—so that every one of them might share in the event.

Lyon's wife, born Beulah Chittenden, the Vermont governor's daughter who married Lyon after he was widowed, protested, saying that no one but she should pay the fine. From her satchel she drew fifty $20 gold coins, sixty silver dollars, and the additional 96 cents in silver and copper coins, turned them over to the U.S. marshal, received a receipt for the $1060.96, and demanded the immediate release of her husband. Matthew, already standing in the doorway of the jail, thanked his friends for their efforts on his behalf, then, quick as a flash, jumped into the sleigh, pulled his wife in beside him, called out, "I'm on my way to Congress!", cracked the whip over the horses, and was off.

Being on his way to Congress made him, by the express mandate of the Constitution, privileged from arrest, since the pending indictment did not charge him with treason, felony, or breach of the peace. The marshal, already reaching out the new warrant, was helpless as he stood watching his prisoner disappear on the ice of the river in company with a formidable collection of Green Mountain Boys.

Lyon's journey to Philadelphia was a triumphal procession which, in 1840, a United States congressman who had witnessed it as a boy, described to fellow congressmen: "The Democrats of the day gathered in a great assembly around the jail, an assembly not equalled by any I have ever seen . . . and a voluntary contribution was called for and taken up; but before it could be applied, the fine had been paid . . . As soon as Lyon was at the jail door, he proclaimed he was on his way to Congress. The cavalcade which attended him stopped at my father's house, and all partook of cakes and hard cider in true Democratic style."

All the way to Philadelphia crowds gathered to greet Lyon. It was his vote, he liked to believe, that in 1800 made Jefferson rather than Aaron Burr president when the tied vote was decided in the House of Representatives. Today's news media, discovering that Jefferson had tried to contribute to the payment of Lyon's federal fine, might see in it a scandal. Clearly, though, Lyon was voting according to his long-held convictions.

Lyon capped his career in the House by sending to President Adams, at the very moment of his relinquishing presidential power, a long letter in which he explicitly told his opinion of Adams. By the bulls that redeemed him, Matthew Lyon wasn't going to let any president think he could have the last word.

Vermont was soon to lose this picturesque representative. Possibly thinking a federal court in Vermont might still find a way to prosecute him, or just possibly growing restless, Lyon sold his Fair Haven home and businesses and moved to Kentucky, which state he was presently to represent in Congress. By 1822 he was living in Arkansas, where he died.

Vermont Joins the Union

While Vermonters joined the Revolutionary forces early and with enthusiasm, the state of Vermont itself, as outsiders often seem surprised to learn, was not one of the original group of colonies to revolt officially against Britain. How could it be when it had no status as an independent entity—two of the original thirteen colonies, New York and New Hampshire, being involved in rival claims to the land now called Vermont?

Actually, for some years there was little enthusiasm either among Vermonters or their neighbors in having Vermont become the fourteenth state. By the time the Revolution ended, Vermont was in a better financial position than its neighbors. On January 15, 1777, a convention of delegates from the towns of the Grants meeting at Westminster on the Connecticut River to ponder their future declared "that the New Hampshire Grants of right ought to be and are forever to be considered as a free and independent jurisdiction." The United States Congress, under pressure from New Hampshire and New York, refused to consider being joined by the upstart jurisdiction.

Snubbed by Congress, Vermont announced itself an independent republic, establishing a postal service and issuing copper coins from the Harmon mint in the town of Rupert. Meanwhile Congress began to grow alarmed as information leaked out that the Allens were negotiating with the British in Canada—which negotiations, if successful, might end with a long alien finger pointing south into the Union. This was something the British had vainly striven to arrange for themselves during the war. Vermonters made it clear they had no great eagerness to sacrifice their cherished independence for the privilege of adding a fourteenth star to the flag of the United States.

Finally, in 1789, when George Washington, always much admired by Vermonters, became president, opposition to joining the Union weakened. There remained, though, one stumbling block, the still unresolved status of the New York grants. The United States Supreme Court might judge them valid as had once the New York Supreme Court. If validated, those grants would automatically invalidate all grants made by New Hampshire Governor Wentworth. The New York claims, originally valued at $600,000, were finally settled by Vermont for the sum of $30,000. Thus, on March 4, 1791, Congress could declare that Vermont be received into the Union "as a whole and entire member of the United States."

The flag had its fourteenth star.

3

The Settlers

In the days of the Green Mountain Boys most of today's Vermont was wilderness, broken only here and there by the settlers' clearings, hard-won from that wilderness. Except for the men who undertook to establish homes there, the region was unknown.

In 1808 a geography published in England described the area:

> a vast country, situated east of New Hampshire, south of Massachusetts and west of New York. It is one hundred and fifty-five miles in length and sixty in breadth. The capital of the State is Bennington.
>
> The Allens are the chiefs, or head men of the country. It is governed by its own laws, independent of Congress and the States . . . The people had for a long time no other name than Green Mountain Boys.

For nearly fifty years people had been making their difficult ways into that unknown vast country which, despite the above weird geographical description, really existed. To these people Vermont's soil seemed highly desirable, especially when compared with the sandy, infertile soils of Connecticut, Rhode Island, and western Massachusetts—desirable enough, in fact, for them to set forth, often with families, to make homes in the unbroken wilderness.

Getting to the Grants

During the 1860s, the historian of Ferrisburg, on the eastern shore of Lake Champlain, told how one family made the journey:

> Among the original proprietors, most of whom were inhabitants of Dutchess County, N.Y., were several of the Field family. When the [town] charter was obtained, their father had taken "rights," as they were termed, for each of his sons, with the exception of one who chose a new saddle in preference to the right of 400 acres, the price being the same for each, $7.50.

The Fields' Journey

> On the first of May, 1786, the family, consisting of the parents and eight children (to one of whom, Mr. Benjamin Field, I am indebted for this account), left Tarrytown, on the Hudson, in a small sailing vessel, which took them up the river as far as Half-Moon Point . . . and from there to the south end of Lake George they went in an ox-cart. At Lake George, they found a man who had built a boat there for the purpose of transporting himself and effects to Grand Isle, and arranged with him to take them to Great Otter Creek. Arrived at the lower end of Lake George, a settler who was erecting a saw-mill there, drew their boat and goods across to Lake Champlain with his oxen, where they again embarked. The wind soon arose, and the boat being so heavily laden that they could not keep her free from water, they were obliged to land on the east shore of the lake and encamp for the night. The next morning was calm and they resumed their voyage down the lake to the mouth of the Great Otter Creek and up that stream to Vergennes, where they landed on the 15th of May, having been 15 days on a journey that is now accomplished in as many hours.

The Strongs' Journey

To get to any grant near the shores of Lake Champlain, that lake route offered the best way, summer or winter. Twenty years earlier the Strong family of Salisbury, Connecticut, was heading for their own grant in Addison, about seven miles south of Vergennes and Great Otter Creek. In 1765 John Strong had visited his grant and there erected the cabin that was to shelter his family when they should accompany him thither. They started north in the following

February, the month chosen so that he might arrive in time to sow crops. With his wife, three children, and household goods, he took the route via Albany, across the Hudson to Fort Gurney, then on the frozen surface of Lake George to Ticonderoga, to reach Addison by crossing the ice of Lake Champlain (probably at the point where it is narrowest, near Crown Point).

> He at once commenced chopping a fallow, and as soon as spring opened, corn and potatoes were planted, and the clearing kept on to be ready for winter wheat. About the first of June he was taken with chills and fever (fever ague) but a wife and children were dependent on his exertions, far away from resources. Kind neighbors had come in but they were no better off than himself. So, when the fit came on, he would lie down by a log heap until it was partly over, and then up and at it again.

Chills and fever—malaria—were then strangely common along the marshy shores of Lake Champlain.

On the far side of Vermont, settlers were using water transportation, too, along the Connecticut River and its tributaries insofar as they might serve. In between, horseback or human back had to serve, with, for the occasional prosperous settler, ox-carts where some kind of a road had been made by cutting the trees. Even this was no easy way and, for all, harder was yet to come.

Settling the Grants

In 1786, in Vergennes, the Fields were laboring. During their "first season, they cleared ten acres and sowed it with wheat, and their labor was repaid by a bountiful harvest . . . they had their flouring done at Vergennes. The creek had to be crossed in boats, as there was no bridge there at the time, and on one occasion when Benjamin went to the mill he attempted to cross too near the Falls and barely escaped being carried over."

To the north in Franklin County, four young bachelors were opening up their own land some ten years later. The son of one of those bachelors, Ephraim Adams, later told of their work:

> My father with three other young men, all from New Ipswich, N.H., in the spring of 1796, purchased 1000 acres of land in Knight's Gore, now in the east part of Bakersfield, worked three seasons; kept bachelor's hall; went back to N.H. each winter, and taught school, returning in the spring. They cleared land, raised winter wheat, and had wheat to sell . . . They had a cow which ran in

the woods—kept from straying by a slash fence [the piled-up slash from their clearing, of course]. As soon as the wheat would do to cut, they boiled and ate it with milk; went to Cambridge to mill; built a stone oven and plastered it with mud. Each slept in an elm bark wrapped about the shape as when on the tree; said that when they went to bed, they were well tucked up. One of them was waked by a mouse making a nest in his hair . . .

An old man told me . . . "your father would carry a pack nigh about as big as folks would think it safe to put into a one horse wagon nowadays." The fourth year my father married.

With the income from teaching and from the wheat flour they could sell, such young bachelors were making sure they were not entering upon married life burdened with heavy debts as, too often, were men with young families. A man like the father of Benjamin Field, with sturdy sons to help with the clearing, also had an advantage.

The Scottish Contingent

In Caledonia County along the Connecticut River, settlers might arrive by the river route. In Barnet, a Colonel Alexander Harvey had, by 1774, bought 7000 acres of land at 14 pence per acre. The ask-

ing price having been 18 pence and Colonel Harvey's first offer one shilling per acre, the 14 pence was a settlement decidedly to the Scotchman's advantage—his total expenditure for the 7000 acres being 408 pounds, 6 shillings, and 8 pence. Immediately he cleared some land, sowed grain, planted potatoes and beans, then took time to prepare logs for his houseraising, which took place on June 11, 1774.

"The town of Ryegate," some ten miles to the south of Barnet, "was chartered by New Hampshire to Rev. John Witherspoon D.D. September 8, 1763. In the winter of 1773, a company was formed of farmers, in the vicinity of Glasgow, Scotland, for the purpose of purchasing a tract of land for settlement in North America. This company was called the Scotch-American Company of Farmers."

The first group of these farmers sailed from Greenock on March 25, 1773, and arrived in Philadelphia on May 24. There, Dr. Witherspoon, president of "New Jersey College" (now Princeton), met them. He "informed them that he had a township called Ryegate, in the province of New York [during the ten years since he first received his grant, the courts had upheld New York's claim] on the Connecticut River, containing about 23,000 acres, which, if they could not suit themselves elsewhere, he would be glad to sell to them . . ."

> After spending five months in exploring the country, north and south, they returned to Dr. Witherspoon, then in Princeton, N.J., and bargained for one half the town of Ryegate. On coming to New York, they met with James Henderson, a carpenter and one of their shipmates, who had been sent to assist them in their undertaking. Leaving Mr. Henderson to come in a sloop by way of Hartford, with their chests, tools, and other necessary articles, they left New York on the 19th of October, and arrived in Newbury, Vt., November 1 . . . One week after their arrival, James Henderson appeared in a canoe [apparently having had to abandon the sloop at the falls in Brattleboro] freighted with the chests and tools aforesaid . . . The town of Ryegate was then divided. The south half fell to the Scotch American Company. This was considered preferable to the north half.

What made the south half seem preferable was, first, that the kind and luxuriance of vegetation suggested that the land there must be more fertile than in the northern half. Secondly,

> It is nearest to provisions which we have in plenty within three to four miles, and likewise within six miles of a grist

mill, and two miles of a saw mill, all of which are great advantages to a new settlement. 3. We have several brooks with good seats for mills, and likewise Wells river runs through part of our purchase, and has water enough for a grist mill at the driest season of the year, of which the north part is almost entirely destitute. 4. We are within six miles of a good Presbyterian meeting.

When they arrived in Ryegate, they found John Hyndman, one of their own countrymen, who had with his family moved into town a few months before. He was engaged in building a house. "So," confesses the canny Scotchman's journal, "we helped him up with it, both for the convenience of lodging with him till we built one of our own, and also that he might assist us in building ours." These houses, built of logs and roofed with strips of hemlock bark, were finished about the first of January, 1774.

"The rest of the winter was spent in making an opening in the wilderness, the whole of the town being covered with trees of various kinds, among which were beech, maple, hemlock, spruce, birch and pines. James Henderson was employed part of the time in manufacturing wooden bowls, dishes, and other articles for domestic use. James Whitelaw went to Portsmouth (N.H.) and Newburyport (Mass.) [a round trip of over 300 miles] for a sleigh load of such necessaries as they needed. In the month of April, they made 60 pounds of sugar . . . In May, Whitelaw commenced the survey of the company's half of the town." A sleigh could move more easily and faster over the then so crude roads than could any kind of cart. But May, with the snows melted, was the time for going through the woods for surveys.

More settlers, arriving on May 23, drew lots for their parcels of land. By 1775, a gristmill had been built and put into operation. A sawmill was operating in July, 1776. Power installations were as important then as today.

The year 1776 was not conducive to settling easily into a life of peace and security. "A message was received that St. Johns [to the northwest and across today's Canadian line] was retaken by the British, and that the Indians, who were a terror to all the early settlers, would be sent in to lay waste the country." While families were hastily removed to the protection of a fort in Newbury, the menfolk returned to Ryegate to cultivate and protect their crops, upon which the lives of all might presently depend. There was no raid and gradually the families drifted back home.

There were no bridges and no roads but spotted trees. When they went to the mill which was in Newbury 10 miles distant, they carried their grists on their backs. This was also the mode of conveyance in carrying articles to and from the store, which was also located in Newbury. There, too was their place of worship. Not only men but women also travelled all that distance on foot that they might have the opportunity of worshipping the God of their fathers in public congregation. "When the ladies," says Mr. Powers, "came to Wells River (there being no canoe), they would bare their feet and trip it along as nimbly as a deer, the men generally went barefooted, the ladies certainly wore shoes."

Wore them to meeting, that is:

Across the state, in Hubbardton, one elderly farmer would reminisce, "Shoes were very scarce and hard to be obtained; thus the children went barefoot in summer among the stubs, and many of them all winter. The writer, at 12 years old, wore all winter the flank of a hide gathered up moccasin-like; and the first pair of boots he ever had was in the winter after he was 20." Even so, the boot legs were so short that, to keep the snow out, he bound pieces of woolen cloth around his legs, using string for binding.

Boots were not then purchasable from stocks in stores but were made in the home from home-grown hides by itinerant shoemakers who progressed from family to family, remaining with each until all needed shoes were finished. Starting with the father of the family, the cobbler sewed boots for each son in turn, the youngest being the last to be shod. In a family with eight grown boys where the shoemaker arrived in September, the youngest one was once heard to complain that by the time his own shoes were made, his feet were pretty cold.

The Settlers' Dwellings

The first must was a cabin, for everywhere in the grants winter could be harsh—nowhere harsher than in Caledonia County, once described as "being a first-rate place for sleigh rides, for the reason that we have nine months of winter and the other three very late in the fall."

Burke, in the northern part of that county, was receiving settlers from Litchfield, Connecticut, as early as 1794. "Almost the whole of the first inhabitants of the town followed the pursuit of agriculture . . . During many years, the inhabitants lived in cabins built of logs, and covered with bark peeled from spruce trees [elsewhere elm or hemlock] and were often doomed, especially in the winter seaons, to endure cold and hunger; for, being poor, they had not the requisite means to procure comfortable clothing to screen themselves and families properly from the rigors of a northern climate . . . sleeping on straw beds or skins of animals at night, in the upper loft of their bark-covered cabins whose roofs, by the influence of the sun's rays, would poorly shield them from the rain or snow or the blasts of a wintry storm." (As bark dried, the edges curled up to leave wider and wider cracks.)

These cabins might have no chimney save a few boards fastened together in a conical form through which to convey the smoke. "Sometimes they would have backs, as they were called, built against the logs at one end of their dwelling, but many were destitute of this appendage." The appendage, described in a bit more detail by the Hubbardton writer, was "a back of stone, laid up." "Their log houses," he said, "were apt to smoke . . . so after a while, they would build from the beams out with split sticks laid cobhouse fashion; and plastered well with clay inside." One cut above the conical wooden chimneys! "Oftentimes these wooden chimneys would take fire."

> It was difficult to get their split-log floor level, so that their home-made table would be one side higher than the other, and the porridge dish could not be full; this they remedied by putting a chip under the edge. For their winter fires they would cut a tree one and a half or two feet through, (the larger the better) cut it up 6 or 8 feet long (there was plenty of wood and the men and boys liked to chop it); after getting these logs to the door, and placing them on rollers [smaller logs] with the axe stuck fast into one end, the two largest boys would put shoulder to shoulder, with their hands hold of the axe helve, and draw; and perhaps a boy and one or two girls pushing behind, all with ruddy, laughing countenances. Having drawn it before the fire-place, it is rolled on, and another nearly as large rolled on top, and a third is placed on long stones in front—the fire is now laid on, with dry kindlings and other small wood until, perhaps, one-fourth of a cord might be on it at a time, thus they had a fire that with little attending to would last 24 hours in the coldest of weather.

Sometimes it would turn out that the "little attending to" was a mistake.

A new settler needed the shelter a cabin could supply and he needed to have his family living there so that settling could go on without interruption. Brick was not to be had where there were no brick kilns. Stone for a fireplace might have to be hauled from a distance, then lifted to considerable heights if a finished chimney was to be built. A perilous wooden chimney seemed, at first, the only alternative.

Fire on the Hearth—and Off

For all, though, fire was as precious as it could be destructive. To Tunbridge, in 1785, came young Deacon Elijah Tracy with his wife and child. They "stopped a week or so with Mr. Morgan's family . . . Carrying a few articles of food and furniture, from day to day, he continued his tedious work [of clearing land and building his cabin] until his excellent wife, impatient to share the toils of her husband, says, 'Elijah, it is too bad for you to travel so far night and morning; I can cook the food and help you a little . . . you take the child and I will take a brand of fire.'" (The brand was to make certain, of course, a fire in the new cabin might be lighted without delay.)

> She had faithfully guarded the firebrand she had taken from Morgan's and now kindled the first fire . . . Furniture they had but little; . . . the Deacon prepared to fix up a table while his wife should cook the dinner. There was a stump in the cabin which could not very well be removed when he had made his house, and it made a good foundation for a table . . . all their furniture consisted of the rude table, one kettle, a bedstead [consisting of a folding frame of perforated lengths of wood which were roped together, then mattressed with a sack full of corn husks] and a few pieces of crockery. In this kettle our housekeeper fried her meat, and then washed it out to make her tea, and the potatoes roasted in the ashes being done, Divine blessing was implored and the little family sat down to eat the first meal in their own house. Mrs. Tracy used to tell her daughters [from one of whom the account came] that she never enjoyed a cup of tea as she did this.

Ironically, the fire which Mrs. Tracy so carefully guarded as she walked to her new home would, a few months later, destroy that home entirely. Nothing daunted, settler Tracy promptly raised a newer and better home.

In 1786, Jehiel Johns—as his son would recount nearly eighty years later—was moving to Huntington from Manchester, a distance of some ninety miles, "bringing wife and movables by way of [the banks of] Otter Creek to Lake Champlain, following . . . by land up the Winooski River to Richmond, and here leaving his companion in the hospitable care of Joel Brownson, one of the new settlers there, he proceeded, with axe on shoulder and such other necessaries as new settlers require, by marked trees through the woods to his pitch in the then unbroken wilderness of New Huntington [20 miles or so east of the Lake] . . . where he proceeded to fell the trees over some two or three acres and then to lay up the body of a log cabin

. . . rolling together, notching and laying the timbers of the lower half unassisted by other human mortal . . . passing the lonely nights which he was obliged to spend in the woods by kindling a fire between two logs and laying down near it on a quantity of soft brush with a blanket and sky over him." Two opportunely arriving passersby helped him to raise the upper half of his cabin. As usual, bark strips roofed it and oiled paper served as windowpanes.

Jehiel Johns remained on his land, to improve it and to raise a more comfortable dwelling when a sawmill was available to make planks. Some so-called settlers soon gave up and moved west—"west" then meaning the Winooski Valley and the shores of Lake Champlain. However, people who stayed put soon had neighbors to lend helping hands.

> In Hinesburg, about ten miles southeast of Burlington, John Weed built a log house . . . and moved into it in 1792. In November, 1797, it was burned with his winter's provision and most of the clothing for the family. At night, while the ruins were yet blazing, his neighbor, Epraphas Hull, mounted his horse and before morning had visited most of the families in town and invited them to come to Mr. Weed's assistance. They did come, bringing timber, boards, nails, tools, provisions, clothing and skillful, willing hands. Before the sun shone, the material for a small house was on the spot, and at night the house was built, finished and furnished. We cannot say how well, but it served the family many years, and is still [1861] a tenant house on the farm.

Such unfortunately not infrequent occurrences finally inspired some resourceful settlers to invent a squirt gun for shooting water at burning walls, for, with the strange chimneys they installed, fires were a frequent occurrence and a provident householder kept his squirt gun within reach at all times. A squirt gun in the cabin could, however, do little for a barn fire. In 1795, "Mr. Stephen Hollister's barn was burned by sparks blowing from a neighbor's clearing. The neighbors who rallied at the burning determined that he should have a new barn. They scattered to invite others and to return with tools, team, provisions &c., next morning . . . The timber was cut, hewed, framed and raised in a day; and before the ruins were done smoking, a new barn frame, 30 by 40 feet, was ready for covering."

The log houses, of course, were never intended to be permanent dwellings—not for the thrifty and hardworking part of the population, at least. An elderly Hubbardton farmer, reminiscing about the early days, wrote: "After a while their log-houses began to decay. Sawmills coming into use, they began to build frame houses, generally of one story with a chimney in the middle 10 or 12 feet square, with three fire places and a large oven [one on each face]. The kitchen fire place was a large one, with a heavy iron-crane with hooks to hang pots and kettles upon: the crane was quite a convenience, for it swung out into the room."

Iron cook-stoves were not even available until 1820 had come, and for long after that were not easily to be had.

Before 1800, though, even without iron stoves and modern plumbing, fine homes were being built in southern Vermont, at least. In March, 1801, Justice Royall Tyler wrote a detailed description of the home he had just bought in Brattleboro, a town that had been chartered in 1753:

The farm consists of 150 acres . . . we have wheat and rye now in the ground . . . we have two large orchards and two smaller ones . . . expect to cut hay enough to winter 30 head of cattle. [He then told of sheep, lambs, geese, turkeys and hens, and went on with the details of the house itself] . . . a handsome portico, two handsome front rooms well finished, papered and painted; and two handsome chambers over them; back is a sitting room and by the side of it a room for my office, which has a door into the sitting room and another out of doors, so that ingress may be had independent of the house; back of the sitting room a good kitchen, from whence you go into two bedrooms, one for the boys and the other for the maids [his daughters], and overhead a meal granary; and over the sitting room an apartment for our hired man and boys; back of the kitchen is a long wood-house, about 20 feet of which makes a summer workroom, and here stands the water-trough, constantly supplied with plenty of excellent water. In front of the house is the fruit garden.

On one side was the kitchen garden and on the other a flower garden—all in all, quite an advance over the settlers' cabins of not so many years before.

4

The Men

Whether the settler made his home in northern Caledonia County or in Bennington or Brattleboro practically on the Massachusetts line, life for him and his family was far from easy. Even in Bennington, or Brattleboro, in the early 1800s, most men were living by agriculture and "farming implements were then few, and of a coarse character such as would now [the 1860's] be discarded from use at once." Meanwhile, especially in remoter counties and until the first crop of grain could mature, the men "were generally obliged to buy their grain of farmers in adjoining towns. The manner of payment was almost universally by days' work, in which they were rich, and possessed of but little else which they could spare . . . 'I tell you we saw hard times,' said Nathaniel Belknap of Goshen when 76 years old. 'The young folks now-a-days couldn't begin to stand it as we did. I moved into my log-house here in the woods when there was but one board on it, and that I brought from New Hampshire.' 'And for weeks after,' said Mrs. Belknap, 'I could lie abed and count the stars.' Said the old man, 'I have been more than a mile beyond Pittsford village to buy a bushel of corn. I couldn't find it between here and there. When I paid for it, I had to take five pecks [over 60 pounds] because I couldn't make change. I took it and started for the mill; got it ground; shouldered it, and carried it home. But,' he added, 'I didn't get off the bed the next day!'" The person reporting this conversation added, "He had travelled at least twenty-six miles that day, and thirteen with 5 pecks of grain on his back. He took a job of lumbering in Pittsford; bought a yoke of oxen, and calculated to work his way through the winter and have a team in the spring; but his oxen sickened and died and he lost his cow before spring."

In those days, "the man who could not carry a hundred pounds on his back ten or twelve miles was hardly fit to begin a new settlement. Nevertheless, if a man prospered sufficiently to acquire a horse, he was quite willing to shift the burden, especially when the load was salts [potash made from wood ashes]. Many a horse's back and sides was made sore in carrying these salts in bags to market," especially if it rained and the lye solution ran down the poor beast's flanks. All this had to be, for money was scarce and nearly everything that a man earned from crops, furs, and potash had to go for taxes which, though they would look small today, were actually a heavy burden.

Potash

Women did their share, and more, in the preparing of potash for market. "Said an aged woman who formerly lived in Lunenburgh, 'I have sat up more nights to boil salts than I am years old. My husband carried them to St. Johnsbury [20 miles] on his back to get something to eat. I was obliged to make baskets and turn every way to keep my children from starving.'" Before even starting in to boil, she would have had to leach the salts from hardwood ashes, by putting them in a hollowed-out log and covering them with water. Hours later, she would boil the liquid down in a 12- to 14-gallon kettle (probably borrowed) "to a consistence called 'salts of lye.'" In St. Johnsbury, these brought $3 to $4 per hundredweight.

A more optimistic view of the settler's lot is described by a writer with the soul of a real estate speculator:

> In a new settlement, the first business of the hus-
> bandman is to cut down the woods, to clear up the lands,
> to sow them with grain; to erect the necessary buildings
> and to open the roads . . . One hundred acres of land in a
> new town does not generally cost him more than the
> wages of one or two years . . . When he comes to apply
> his labor to his own land, the first crop of wheat will
> generally pay him for all the expense he has been at in
> clearing up, sowing and fencing his land, and at the same
> time increases the value of his land eight or ten times the
> original cost.

Had that writer lived another 75 years to visit the thriving farms of Mt. Holly, he might have thought with another writer:

> Since the building of the railroad through the town, wood and lumber have been important items of traffic and the remark is often made by farmers that if their farms were now in their primitive condition, with the timber all standing, they would be worth more than they now are, with all the buildings and other improvements . . .
>
> The hardy pioneers, while felling the trees, and laboring day and night to pile and burn them, little thought that the time would come when the timber, which it cost them so much toil and labor to get rid of, would, if standing, be worth more than their farms, with all the improvements of three-fourths of a century.

Pound Cake

The first mechanical device on record among the settlers was the "plumping mill" for pounding the corn they grew. In Bolton, not too far, as the crow flies, from Huntington, ex-Revolutionary soldier Samuel Barnet rolled up his cabin, made the usual clearing, and sowed corn and some other grain. Next came the plumping mill. On the top of a large stump he made a small fire and left it to burn until the stump was "burned out hollow, like a mortar. A heavy plunger was then attached to a long spring pole [a sapling] in such a manner that when the operator pulled it down upon the corn in the mortar, the spring pole would lift it out. In such mills the corn was prepared for bread . . . they never pounded more than enough for one meal at a time; so the sound of plumping mills were heard in the morning, pounding corn for breakfast cake, then at noon, and again it heralded the supper hour, and was musical to the pioneers, for the sound of these mills could be heard a long distance, and the settlers scattered here and there found its echo among the hills a more cheerful sound than the howling of wolves." Some wag dubbed the eventual product "pound cake."

The Women

For the women especially, this reminder that there were other "human mortals" was comforting even when they were too busy just keeping that wolf from the door to visit back and forth. "The women and girls knew how to, and actually did, milk cows, feed pigs and poultry, make butter and cheese, carry wood and water, and sweep house with a broom made by their fathers or brothers from ash or birch sticks." They were lucky, at the beginning, if they had such things as cows, pigs, and poultry to care for. The wives were further occupied with bearing children at about two-year intervals.

Also, until the 1820s, when an occasional cook-stove made its appearance in homes, all meals were prepared before open fires or in great brick ovens. Potatoes might be roasted in the coals, thus avoiding the use of a pot. Dried corn might be soaked and boiled, or porridge made from various grains or beans. "Tea and coffee were unknown . . . broths of various kinds—corn, bean, and barley— were in constant use. In many families, hasty pudding with milk, if milk could be had, was almost the standing supper."

The Livestock

Another writer reminisced: "At that time, most of the inhabitants owned but one cow, and for many years the only pasture which they had for their cattle consisted of the forest, and not infrequently they would ramble to a considerable distance, in which case the only guide their owner had in seeking them was the sound of a bell, fastened with a leather strap to the neck of a cow." Green shrubs and the grass springing up in an occasional forest glade formed the cow's diet from which to manufacture the milk so needed by her owner's family. Presumably, if one man's cow became dry, a neighbor might help by supplying milk until the new calf was born. So there had to be an occasional unaltered bull in the vicinity. Otherwise male calves were castrated to provide the needed work oxen, one account listing a cow as worth from $12 to $15 while a pair of oxen could bring from $50 to $60.

Usually it was one of the womenfolk who went out after a nonreturning cow, for the loss of a cow and her milk could be a real disaster. One woman told of walking until night fell, then seeking shelter in some distant cabin before finally locating her errant cow by morning's light and driving her the many miles home. There was always a chance the cow or, more frequently, sheep might never return, particularly if wolves or bears had found them. Bears, at least, might offer compensation "as their flesh, many times, served in part to furnish the inhabitants with meat, which from domestic animals was very scarce, and their skins used for moccasins and various other purposes," such as fur rugs or bed coverings.

Making Clothes from Scratch

An old-timer of Hubbardton reminisced:

> In those days women manufactured the cloth with
> which they and their families were clothed; knit the stock-
> ings for themselves, their husbands and sons, as well as

leggins for the latter, as boots were not known for boys; did their own housework and made up the clothing for their families.

The young women understood how to spin and weave wool, flax and tow. Every young lady who could procure it by her own labor, had one calico dress. A few years since, a matron lady was living in town, who when young worked at spinning and weaving for 50 cents a week, to enable her to purchase a calico dress at a dollar a yard. Thus it took the labor of two weeks to pay for one yard; and as 6 yards constituted a pattern, it required 12 weeks' work to pay for her dress, besides the making and trimming.

About 150 miles to the northeast of Hubbardton, another elderly citizen reminisced in a similar vein:

Among my earliest recollections is the buzz of the wheel and the thumping of the old loom; and whenever there came a sunny day in March, the flax-break might be heard at almost every farmer's barn, and very well do I recollect the big bunches of woolen and linen yarns which ornamented the kitchen of the old homestead, spun by my mother and sisters . . . In addition to making all the cloth for clothing the family, she made hundreds of yards of woolen and linen cloth, and exchanged it in the store for family necessaries [at a time when corn and rye grains brought 50 cents a bushel, oats 20 cents, potatoes 12 to 20 cents also a bushel]. Nearly all the clothing was made at home, being sewn by hand.

Cotton cloth was then an article of luxury. Even in Bennington, close to the Massachusetts line, "nearly all the cloth in use by our people was made by hand labor in families, from wool and flax, the production of their farms. The wool was carded by hand by the farmers' wives and daughters [a card resembled a large, oblong wire hairbrush with short bristles set in parallel rows] and spun into yarn upon the 'great wheel,' and then woven into flannel by them or, being doubled and twisted and properly dyed, was made into coverlets for beds . . .

"The flax, after being retted in the field [left in the field for moisture and rot to separate the fibers from the remainder of the stems], was prepared . . . for the further work of the family. Here the hetchel separated the tow from the finer flax . . . the flax being wound upon the distaff was spun upon the 'little wheel' which was turned by means of a footboard and made into linen yarn. This yarn, being woven into cloth, was used for sheets and pillow-cases, tablecloths, towels and under-garments, in short for nearly all the purposes for which purchased linen and cotton cloth are now [1860s] employed. The tow, spun upon the large wheel, made filling for linen warp and furnished a coarse article for the common uses of linen cloth." By 1801, the first carding machine, "lessening the labor of the house-wife by one-third," was installed in North Bennington. More such machines were bound to appear all over the state, though hardly in time to be of much use to Mrs. Jane Hazelton of Newfane.

Of Mrs. Hazelton, it was claimed that she was "the first white woman and undoubtedly the oldest person that ever lived in town . . . who died Feb. 16, 1810, at the advanced age of 103 years, 11 months, 11 days. A venerable lady who well remembers the cente-narian says of her, that the day she was 100 years old she spun a full day's work, and then called her son and told him to set her wheel away, as she had spun her last thread."

A woman's work was practically never done. Though her daughters might grow to be of considerable help, their skills were bound to attract the attention of young men in need of companions and housekeepers. Once married, the quality of a girl's work—the bread she baked, the thread she spun, the cloth she wove, the way she kept house—was bound to reveal the quality of her mother's training.

The clothes worn by all the family were equally revealing of the housewife's skill. Thus, "when it is considered that nearly all of this clothing was made up in the home, and that the mother also thought it part of her duty to give her daughters instruction in cookery and other branches of housekeeping, some idea may be formed by the young ladies of the present day [1860s] of the active labors to which their grandmothers were subjected."

Their own workaday clothing was simple: "They were clad, when engaged in their work, which was nearly all the time, on week-days in short gown and petticoat of some coarse material, with a striped apron—calico being quite a dressy article" and reserved for Sun-day-go-to-meeting clothes, if a woman was fortunate enough to own such.

What They Ate

The kind of food cooked depended upon the agricultural and hunting skills of the men. With tea and coffee practically unknown, broths made from corn, beans, or barley were frequently prepared. From Dummerston, in Vermont's southeast corner, comes a rather detailed description of the early settlers' diet:

> In all the New England settlements, one common article of food was bean porridge. It was eaten for breakfast and

oftentimes for supper. Dinner usually consisted of boiled meat and some kind of vegetables, most frequently turnip. These were boiled in a large iron pot or kettle.

To make bean porridge, a sufficient quantity of beans was boiled with meat and turnip. When these were removed, the residue, with the beans, was made into porridge. In cold weather enough was made at once to last several days [being reheated each day]. After milk became plenty, that, with brown bread, was eaten, usually, by families for their evening meal. The brown bread was baked in a stone or brick oven often built separate from the house. On baking days, when the oven was sufficiently heated, the coals were removed with the "fireslice," and the oven swept clean with the "oven broom." The "bread peel," a kind of wooden shovel, was used to place the bread in the oven where it was baked on the bare heated stone or brick. The grandfathers and grandmothers claimed that no bread baked in a pan or dish ever tasted so sweet as it did when baked as they were accustomed to have it done.

Pumpkins were baked in the same way as bread, and also furnished a common article of food. A ripe pumpkin having a very hard shell was taken, and a hole was cut in the stem-end some five or six inches in diameter, the piece being kept whole which was taken out. The seeds and all the stringy substance were then scraped out clean. Thus prepared, it was partly filled with new milk and covered with the piece taken out, placed in a well-heated oven and left to bake six or eight hours. It was allowed to cool in the oven, and, when served, was eaten with milk. Some scraped out the pumpkin and ate it in bowls—others turned the milk into the pumpkin and ate from the pumpkin . . . Pumpkins were very much preferred to squashes by the early settlers, and few of the latter were raised.

Turnips and parsnips were raised in large quantities and were the most common vegetables. Very few potatoes were grown and scarcely a barrel would be disposed of by a large family in a year. Sweet corn, which is so extensively used at the present day [about 1890], was unknown, and when corn was wanted to boil or roast in the green state, yellow flint corn was used. Considerable quantities of wheat were raised, but it was not much used in every-day life. Wheaten cakes were a luxury to be enjoyed when company was present. Barley cakes were eaten and buckwheat was not much relished except as hoe-cakes and "flapjacks." Boiled and baked Indian puddings were a common diet . . . The style of living in "ye" olden time has been celebrated in song.

> Potage and puddings without custards and pies,
> With turnips and parsnips are common supplies;
> We have pumpkins at morning and pumpkins at night,
> 'Twas not for pumpkins, we should be in a plight.

Great quantities of meats were eaten. These consisted of beef and pork and wild meats obtained in the forests, such as bear, deer, moose, wild turkeys and smaller game. The streams and rivers abounded in fish of which large quantities were caught and eaten in many families.

Across the state, in Hubbardton near Lakes Hortonia and Bomoseen, Amos Churchill reminisced of the early days:

> Fish, especially the sucker, was a great accommodation to the early settlers. This kind was plenty and large. In the month of May they would make their appearance at the mouth of the streams; when two or three young men, with a torch and a scoop net, would sometimes haul out a barrel of them in the course of a few hours. These, being dressed, salted and smoked, might be kept good through the season. They would go well as they were, but much better broiled with a little butter, and even if they were kept well packed and salted in a barrel, they were at all times in season for boiling, frying and broiling. And should it happen that there might be a little pork with it, they were excellent with johnny cake and potatoes. The way they smoked them was to get a very limber bush, cut off the twigs, and then hang them [the fish] on the limbs, which being set in the large chimney might be smoked in large quantities at a time. Many a family has been preserved from want by this kind of food.

Actually, except for a young rooster or a hen grown too old to lay eggs, few settlers had much protein food other than such fish or the "wild meats obtained in the forests." Domestic animals, unless injured or too old for other use, were far too valuable, as well as scarce in the early days, to be slaughtered for meat.

The Children

Children, too, had their problems from the beginning. Those large families—occasionally numbering as many as twenty children—did not leave much time for the mother to give attention to each. Bearing and nursing one after another, while continuing to perform the usual duties in house and out, was enough even for the doughty women of early days. Small wonder that early records show that young children sometimes became victims of burnings and scaldings, the latter probably occurring as young hands reached for bubbling kettles swung out from the open fires on cranes.

Another risk, of course, was the danger of getting lost in the almost unbroken wilderness. In Fayston, a boy of four had wandered off into the woods and was not found by searchers until three days later: "This being the second time the men had been called to hunt for lost children in 5 years, some of them were getting tired of the thing, whereupon Ziba Boyce drew up a set of resolutions and read them after the child was found" (safe and sound, fortunately). "It was resolved, 'that mothers be instructed to take care of their children, and not let them wander off into the woods to be food for bears, or for the neighbors to hunt up!'" Clearly, those were the days before the term "male chauvinism" had been dreamt up.

Even before they had grown old enough to share in spinning, weaving, tailoring, cooking, or heavy duties in forest and field, children were expected to take care of themselves in those frequently recurring emergencies which seemed to be most frequent when no elders were at hand.

Facing a Bear

In the spring of 1783, Mr. Marsh, with three children [15-year-old] Elias, "Rene" [12 years] and James [8 years] went to Waterbury, having a horse to carry provision and help them in fording the streams, to find his corn planted the previous year all gone and himself and children with no provisions except what they had brought with them. Using these as sparingly as possible, he planted his corn, and leaving his children with provisions for a week, he returned to Corinth for the rest of the family. At the end of the week, not having provisions for another day, Elias proposed to go down to the falls to catch some trout.

On their way, they found a large bear sitting directly in their path and unmistakeably disputing their passage. Elias had a gun loaded with shot and a large dog. Fearing to discharge the gun at the bear, the dog was let loose upon him, he attacking bruin in the rear, and dodging out of the way when bruin turned to repay the compliment; thus by cautious advance on the part of Elias and the dog, the bear was backed out of the way and the children allowed to proceed.

Their next obstacle was the Waterbury river, the only means of crossing which was a small tree lying across. Elias carried James on his back; but Rene, trying to walk across with Elias to steady her, became dizzy and fell into the stream. She sunk twice, but was finally rescued by Elias, yet so nearly drowned as to require the utmost effort to resuscitate her. James was brought back across the river and the two, supporting their sister on either side, slowly made their way to a pile of driftwood which, being set on fire, enabled them to dry their clothes, after which, the day being spent, they returned to their camp.

It must be remembered that setting a pile of wood on fire was then no mean achievement; it was done with flint and steel striking a spark that had to be skillfully nourished into flame.

"The next morning they started for the nearest neighbor [some 10 miles away]. This time Elias carried each of the others across the Waterbury river." They remained with the neighbor until they got word of their now distracted father's return to camp, after an absence of three weeks.

Children Alone

In March, 1784, ex-Revolutionary captain Charles Sias was becoming one of the first settlers of Danville in Caledonia County. "His wife was the first white woman who dared to breast the long and dreary winter of this deep, unbroken wilderness." His young children had to breast it, too. "They reached the log cabin early in the afternoon, dug it out from beneath the snow, which had nearly buried it." Leaving John, aged eleven, in charge of his sisters, Sias drew his handsled the nearly ten miles back to Peacham, planning to return the next day with his wife and the rest of the family, which included seven sons and three daughters. "The snow was very deep, and the way was trackless . . . Mr. Sias, with two men to assist, went forward on snow-shoes, and drew the sled, loaded with the girls, and some goods, the boys following." The mother, as well as her daughters, rode the handsled. "In three days more the effects were all removed and the lone family began the hard labors on the wilderness."

Soon, with the first inkling of spring, sap began to run in the maple trees and the Sias family joined forces in collecting and boiling down sap for sugar. Partly this product went for family consumption, partly it was bartered so that other, still more essential items might be obtained.

The Sias children just might have thought this winter's settling in was fun and found the wearisome watching of boiling sap, so that it might not scorch, a delightful challenge. But always in the backs of

their minds they were painfully aware that a new day might bring a new kind of emergency which they themselves must manage to meet, possibly without the help of their elders.

Such an emergency faced the Marsh children in Waterbury and they met it resourcefully. Such an emergency faced Solomon Story when the falling tree crushed the life out of his father. The fourteen-year-old boy, without help or advice, simply set to work chopping up the log so that its sections were not too large for him to roll unaided.

Reviving an Injured Father

A similar kind of emergency faced the son of Jonas Boutelle, one of the early settlers in Franklin County. Jonas

was hurt by the fall of a tree while at work with Mr. Eli Bell, browsing cattle, quite a distance from home. He was reported dead, and neighbors rallied to bring him home. When they arrived, he was breathing. His eldest son James, quite young, being left with his father, had blowed in his mouth, causing him to catch breath; and, with remarkable presence of mind, had been a few rods to a spring, obtained water, wet his father's face and put a little in his mouth. Mr. B. was not fully conscious until Dr. Hall had operated on his skull and dressed the wound . . . The distance travelled to get the doctor, to and back, was 42 miles.

A Social Emergency

An emergency of quite another and, fortunately, less serious nature was dealt with successfully by little Sally Morse, aged twelve, of Groton, in Caledonia County.

> In the year 1799, it being the day of the annual parade and drill of Capt. Morse's military Company some miles from his residence, where his wife lay sick of fever, with Sally, then only 12 years of age, her only attendant. At 11 o'clock A.M., Jonathan Macomber, the captain's confidential friend, appeared "with orders from the captain" to lay the cloth for 40 guests, who would dine with him that day at 1 o'clock P.M. Nothing daunted, Sally at once pressed Macomber into serving as "chopper of wood and drawer of water," and when the appointed hour arrived, bringing the captain and his 40 military guests, the order was obeyed to the letter.

Captain Thomas Morse (1764–1843) was born in Groton, Massachusetts, and became a first settler of Groton, Vermont, in 1783 or 1784. He built the first mill, raised the first frame house, and the first hill of corn to be raised in that town was on his land. Sally, it appears, was a worthy daughter of that father.

Education

Those obviously quick-witted and self-reliant people who had moved into the grants were determined that their children should have an education. Until a town could boast enough voters to support a school, parents would band together to make such arrangements as they could, using whatever pedagogical material was available.

First Schoolrooms

In Bradford, a thriving town on the Connecticut River, an elderly woman would one day recall that "the first school she ever attended was in her father's barn and was taught by Mary Rogers . . . and that, during school hours one day, an unruly heifer broke into the barn floor among the children, when their mistress with great energy seized the little ones and threw them over into the bay," where they landed safely on top of the hay.

In Marshfield, some seventeen miles to the northeast of Montpelier, "there was a school a number of years in the Dwinell district, before the convenience of a schoolhouse was enjoyed. Four winters this school was kept in Simeon Dwinell's kitchen . . . the house was small and Mrs. Dwinell had eight children of her own. But she doubtless got along nicely, washing days and all. The children must be educated; in those days troops of little ones were not so much in the way."

As late as 1801, Barton had so few voters that, "in the summer, Mr. James May, Dr. Jonathan Allyn and Stephen Dexter employed Mariam Darling of Wheelock to teach in their families, she teaching that summer three months, one month in each family, the oldest child in each going with her and boarding in the other families, each family furnishing two scholars, but the youngest being of too tender age to leave the mother's care, so the school always consisted of four scholars all told." Boarding around, for the teachers at least, would become an old Vermont custom.

By 1801, the town of Marshfield (some 35 miles to the south of Barton) would be ready to reject its first schoolhouse in favor of a bigger, better one. It "set up the old school-house at vendue . . . So the old school-house was sold, a little, square log building, covered with bark; a big stone chimney with an opening above for the smoke to go out and the rain to come in, and the grand old forest for playground, and did it not ring with the merry shouts of childhood? They needed no gymnasium then. Were there not trees to climb, the birds' nests and squirrels to hunt, and partridges and woodchucks to look after?" During school hours, though, the children "had to sit straight, keep their eyes on the book, and their toes on the crack."

Hiel Hollister wrote of the school he attended in Pawlet, on the western border of the state:

> Next to providing themselves a shelter and the most common necessaries of life, our fathers, true to the institutions in which they had been reared, directed their attention to . . . education. Schools were established as soon as a sufficient number of scholars could be gathered in any locality, and the progress of the settlement of the town can better be traced by the *number* of school districts than by any other means. Money being scarce, the better qualified would frequently take turns in teaching with little or no compensation. If nothing better could be had, a deserted log cabin would be fitted up for a school-room and made to answer.

School Routine

Our early schools were limited to the branches of reading, writing, spelling and arithmetic, and it was rare that the latter extended beyond the rule of three. The education of girls was still more limited and it was not common for them to learn arithmetic. By degrees other branches were introduced, and grammar was taught, perhaps, as early as 1810. Those who first learned grammar were considered prodigies . . .

A description of the school house and school in which we received our education from 1811 to 1820, will suffice for most of the schools of that day. A plain plank building of repulsive exterior, having on one end an immense stone chimney, through which there was a great prospect of the sky, and whose cavernous jaws would hold in their embrace a half cord of wood, a writing table running round next the wall, a row of benches in front made of slabs inverted, supported on pins like carpenters' horses, a few low benches in the centre, a desk in the corner next the chimney on which lay the ferule, the emblem of our schoolmaster's authority, and the establishment was complete.

After the fashion of the day, the teacher would call the school to order and detail one of the scholars and invest him with the rule. His duty was to watch the school and pass the rule to the first transgressor of the rules of the school, who relieves guard and passes it on to the next delinquent, and so on, with the comforting assurance that whoever got the rule twice or had it when the school closed should have it applied to his own palm. The plan served its purpose, and order and stillness prevailed . . .

We have seen ridges raised on both the hands of a delicate girl who would laugh in the face of her tormentor, while the cowardly boy would make a loud outcry and be let off easily. It was a matter of principle with the children not to cry if they could help doing so.

But when flagellation failed, we were sometimes required to extend our arm at a right angle with a heavy rule or book in our hand, the master standing near to rap our knuckles if our arm fell below the horizontal line. Or we would be seated on an andiron or a block of wood near the chimney corner, which would be called a dunce-block and the scholars be required to point the finger of scorn at us. But when wholly incorrigible, as a last resort we would be placed between two girls. This would unseal a fountain of tears and force the perspiration through the hide of a crocodile. We wilted then. But alas! such was the hardening nature of this capital punishment that its frequent repetition reconciled us to it, and as we grew older we even began to relish it.

A Brattleboro writer listed a schoolmaster's indispensable qualifications (for the winter term, at least): "He must understand how to make a good pen (out of a goose quill) and have an indomitable will, and sufficient physical power to maintain an absolute monarchy over cabined, cribbed, confined juvenile republicans."

The Pupils

Such "absolute monarchy" was hard to maintain over a crowded schoolroom where the older pupils might possibly rival in age, and would certainly rival in maturity and strength, the schoolteacher. Boys practically grown to manhood got their education only during winter terms when their fathers had less urgent need of their work in field and forest. Older girls also were often kept home during summers when they were needed to gather wild berries and fruit and prepare them for drying or to help prepare meals for large companies of ever hungry field workers. Summer terms were generally for younger children, whom a female teacher was expected to handle.

School Buildings and Equipment

In the center of the state, Randolph's school problems were much like Pawlet's: "The first school district in Randolph was organized in 1794 . . . It was then voted to build a schoolhouse 21 by 16 feet and to be lighted by three windows. Joshua Blodgett was then appointed vendue-master [auctioneer] and the building of the schoolhouse was struck off to Nathan Daves, the lowest bidder, for £29, 10s."

By 1809, the town was agitating for a new schoolhouse. It was still agitating in 1815, when a building committee reported "that, in their opinion, a house 24 feet long and 18 wide would be large enough to contain all the scholars in the district"—then eighty in number. The new specifications included a center door, porch, clapboards, seven windows of twenty lights (panes) each, lath, plaster, and so forth.

It was the custom at the annual school meeting to vote a tax of ⅛ cord of wood to each scholar, or its equivalent at the rate of $2.00 per cord. The wood was yearly brought to the school-house in a green state, and it was not uncommon to be out of wood in mid-winter, on account of the delinquency of some parent to furnish his quota. The wood-shed fared hard on such occasions, being partially stripped of its boards to make fire-wood. About the year 1838, this manner of getting wood was done away with, and the wood has since been got on the grand list [through taxes].

Old-fashioned fire-places were used in the school-house up to the building of the second one [these of the huge size described for some homes and inns]. The district then had a sheet iron stove made expressly for the purpose, which was open in front, or with a large sheet iron shutter before it. The stove pipe was of an oval shape, about 18 or 20 inches wide and about 8 inches thick, and run straight up into the chimney. The scholars used often to shove it up into the chimney and fill it full of wood on cold days, when the teacher would allow of it; and, on one occasion, some of the scholars climbed upon the house and filled the chimney with wood, which raised quite a breeze in school. They never tried the experiment again.

By 1835, Randolph was building another schoolhouse, then yet another in 1866–1867. This latter was a real source of town pride— "an ornament to the district and one that will have a refining influence on the minds of the scholars." Desks had "cast iron trimming and hardwood tops." There were blackboards, reversible seats, a special teacher's desk. Outside there was a canopy and a belfry. It was painted white and, as the 1869 historian proudly described it, "finished off in the nicest manner."

Teachers

The teachers' situation did not improve so quickly or radically. "Boarding around had always been the custom down to recent date." This meant that parents paid their school taxes, in part at least, by keeping the teacher in their homes. "The board was apportioned to each scholar and some poor families with a large number of scholars suffered great inconvenience"—the teacher's inconvenience apparently being taken for granted. "However, the schoolmaster in many instances passed by such families, and those more able bore the burden. Some wealthy men in the district were so strict in the matter of board that, when the teacher's time was up, they were not backward to tell them of it. It is told of one parent, that on a certain occasion, when the schoolmaster's time was just out as they were eating a meal, the man told the master that he was entitled to about half a meal, but he was not disposed to be mean about it and he (the master) might finish it up if he pleased."

In some towns, the pleasant custom of passing the teacher from home to home was continued until late in the century. During the 1860s, light began to dawn and a town like East Highgate on the Canadian border would boast, "at the present time our schools are supported on the grand [tax] list, and teachers have a steady boarding place instead of boarding around as was once the custom."

The teacher, if the district had funds enough to attract one from outside, could be a college student taking time out to earn enough cash either to purchase land for settling or to keep himself in college while he paid for clothes, board and books. "In asking old teachers the wages received," says one account, "their reply was, 'but little more than board.' The story still holds current, that one of these early candidates for schoolmaster's honors, on making application for a school, was asked his terms, and that he, looking at the widemouthed fireplace, answered, 'he thought he could cut the wood and teach the school for the ashes he could make!' " A woman teacher, like Sophronia Littlewood, could not. In 1820, it is recorded, Clarendon Springs voted to pay her "sixty-seven cents per week, in grain, for teaching their school." She, of course, was to find the means of converting it into cash.

"We were not distracted with a multiplicity of class-books," Hollister wrote of his school days. "The last teacher who gave the finishing touches, we recollect was employed at the extravagant price of seven dollars per month of twenty-six days. This may not seem so extravagant, when we consider that our school only numbered from sixty to eighty scholars." In Bradford, about the year 1867, the cost of educating 139 scholars between the ages of 4 and 18 amounted to "about $1000, exclusive of interest on the buildings, which would swell the sum to $1200, or about $9 per scholar." Small wonder that the school superintendent's report then expressed unhappiness with the quality of learning some of the pupils seemed to have received.

Ambitious pupils, or those boasting ambitious parents, might try going on to one of the academies springing up in Vermont towns. In Brandon, there was completed in 1833 a building for an institution that styled itself "The Vermont Literary and Scientific Institute," with classrooms, library, chapel, and 30 dormitory rooms.

Tuition per quarter of 11 weeks was from $.50 to $4.50, depending upon the course of study. A dormitory room was worth $2 per week or, where two pupils shared a room, $1.00 per week each. Board in school came to another $1.00 a week at school, $1.25 in private families where furnished rooms might be secured at very low cost—to our eyes, at least. Rules of the school were very strict but probably no stricter than in many homes. The Institute throve until, much later, the town took it over—as did other Vermont towns with other private academies—to merge it with the public high school.

"It was," wrote Henry Clark of Poultney, "an age of hard work and simple fare, interspersed on the part of the men with trainings, musters, raisings, huskings, wrestling matches, chopping bees and piling bees—and in the female world with quilting, apple-paring and carding bees."

Bees

Young girls were early indoctrinated into the joys and obligations of such bees. From Guilford, comes the account:

> The young girl . . . was taught to sew sometimes when four years old. The odd bits and ends of calico dresses were cut and basted for bed-quilt blocks by the mother and given to Miss to sew. The cover to her quilt she was expected to finish by the time she became marriageable, and it was to be part of her marriage outfit. When the girl had attained somewhere near her majority, eighteen or somewhere near, a quilting was given. All the young ladies of the neighborhood assembled at her house to complete the bed-quilt. Stories and pleasant chat enlivened the busy afternoon, followed by tea, after which the beaux were expected.

If there was no immediate exuse to organize a bee, either for her daughter's or her own quilts, a woman might just decide to make a call on a neighbor:

> They would take with them any little delicacy which they had, if they believed the lady to be called on did not possess it, and then armed with a little-wheel and a good supply of flax, they set out to consummate a long afternoon's chat; or, provided that neither the visitor nor the one to be visited happened, just then, to be favored with a large store of edibles, they often resorted to the bank of the lake, where seated with hook and line, they were soon provided with something presentable to serve up for supper while at the same time they were enabled to proceed undisturbedly with their social enjoyments.

The above quote came from the shores of Lake Champlain. A citizen of Dummerston, near the Connecticut River, agreed: "Their amusements were few but exceedingly social." "Growing naturally out of this," both writers agreed, "was the practice of doing work by 'bees.' If a fallow was to be logged, the invitation was sent round, and a general turnout of men, boys, dogs and oxen was the result"—as, remember, when a neighbor's house had burned down—"and the inevitable bottle added inspiration to the occasion."

Source of Inspiration

"It is granted," the Dummerston citizen told of this habit, "that cold water was used when nothing stronger could be obtained; but strong drinks were much used, and the grandfathers were full of expedients to make them. Malt beer was a common beverage."

> If Barley be wanting to make into malt,
> We must then be contented, and think it no fault;
> For we can make liquor to sweeten our lips,
> Of pumpkins and parsnips and walnut tree chips.

Home-brewed beer and cider that had stood long enough to ferment—"as soon as the people obtained orchards"—were supplemented by still stronger drinks, many early towns boasting several distilleries, undoubtedly of the size of later moonshine stills. Pawlet, for instance, once had five such. In any case, "All drinking of the common people was social, all drinking from the same mug or bowl."

Wrote the Cabot historian (as did the historians of other towns):

No occasion was ever perfect without it. If a neighbor came to make a friendly visit, if the pastor came to make a call, or to join a couple in the holy bonds of matrimony, or perform the last sad rites of burying the dead, and especially when a child was born into the world, the whisky and flip went around merrily; and when the ladies had a quilting bee, every time they rolled the quilt all must take a little toddy, and when they had rolled it about four times, they were ready to drop work, tell stories and have a jolly time. A story is told of one of the good old ladies who at the conclusion of a quilting put on her . . . large, old-fashioned poke bonnet . . . and got it wrong side before, covering her face entirely.

Cabot's first distillery was built in 1809 and within a few years there were twelve distilleries merrily turning out their product:

Cider and whisky were the staple commodity of the times, the former selling for $3 per barrel, and the latter from 67 to 75 cents per gallon . . . No farmer thought of beginning a winter with less than 12 to 15 barrels of cider and one or two barrels of whisky in the cellar. It was no uncommon thing for a young man to hire out for the season for 300 gallons of whisky, and this he could dispose of for stock, store-pay, or anything he could get.

Before 1809, distilling must have been a private venture.

On all public days whisky went around freely, and all officers had to treat. March meeting, 1806, tradition says the whisky was kept in the closet of the schoolhouse where the meeting was held, which was imbibed so frequently by candidates and their supporters, some of them got so they hardly knew which way to vote. About middle way of the proceedings of the meeting, it was voted that the door leading into the closet be shut and kept so for the space of one-half hour.

At another time, a confused justice of the peace once "got a little bewildered and made the groom promise to 'forsake her' and 'cleave to all other women.' " As one historian put it, "The mystery is how any one kept sober; how any one knew whether other people were sober."

How to Keep a Husband Sober

Ethan Allen, who had celebrated the Green Mountain Boys' seizure of Fort Ticonderoga by liberal partaking of the commandant's store of liquor, continued to follow that pattern to a considerable degree until Fanny took a hand in the matter.

It is well understood that she always exerted a very decided influence over her brave yet eccentric husband. She . . . especially desired to reform him for the habit of being out late at night with dissipated company.

It is related of her . . . that she adopted a very ingenious method of restraining him in this matter . . . "I will find out," she said, "whether you come home drunk or sober!" and thereupon she drove a nail—pretty well up—in the wall of the bedroom and said to him: "There, Ethan, when your watch is hanging on that nail in the morning, I shall know that you came home sober."

"Agreed!" says the old hero.

He, however, found it a rather difficult job to prove his good behavior, at all times, by this severe test. When he had taken a drop too much . . . he would make a dash at the nail, but it would dodge him, and the watch ring hit one side—but he would brave up his resolution and nerves and make another sally, and the floor would now give way, or perhaps his knees get out of joint; yet not discouraged, he would stick to it and work up to the nail until he got the ring of his watch fairly hooked, when he would retire satisfied that all would be well with Fanny this time.

If she had a word to say in the morning, he would point his finger to the watch—"Fanny, do you see that? I came home sober last night."

Temperance Threatens

In Cabot, at least, enthusiasm for whisky made from their large crops of potatoes began to wane with the farmers and their families. They "began to think that raising so many potatoes was running out their farms, and after all not so profitable as some other crops, and less were planted, and the number of distilleries decreased until in 1832, there were none running in town."

For a while, rum manufactured in southern New England from West Indian molasses took the place of locally distilled whisky. But "about 1825, the temperance question began to be agitated; people began to think that they could get along without quite so

much stimulant, and from that time to the present [about 1880] there has been a marked diminution in the quantity absorbed in town."

Even before 1825, that year when Lyman Beecher's temperance sermons were published and began to be widely circulated, some citizens were having second thoughts on the subject of providing hard liquor on every social occasion. In 1821, in Waitsfield, "at a 'raising' one of the men, Wheeler by name, became intoxicated . . . fell and was carried home insensible, and found upon examination to have expired."

This accident so startled fellow citizens that when, soon after, Deacon Moses Fisk "sent out invitations to the raising of a barn," he stipulated that no liquor was to be furnished.

"Matters proceeded as usual in such cases, until the moment for raising the ridge-pole, or 'rum pole,' as it was called. The men bent to the task, but strange to say, suddenly found themselves devoid of all strength, and after several trials, gave it up, saying they could do nothing more until strengthened by liquor. It was late in the afternoon, and the master-workman became so nervous that he finally begged the Deacon to allow him, at his own expense, to provide a treat." The deacon, however, stood firm, reminded the company of Wheeler's death, and said firmly, "I cannot do what my conscience forbids me to do, and if this frame cannot go up without rum, every stick of timber shall rot on the ground where it lies." The men, since they really liked the deacon, finally gave in and the barn frame was raised in peace, in contrast to other raisings which were often "scenes of riot and accident."

Mowing Bees

Even when the temperance movement began to take hold, bees were not discontinued, for work had to be done and, in pre-mechanization days, the only way to get it done was by assembling many workers:

> It was no uncommon occurrence for from 5 to 8 acres of heavy timbered land to be logged off in a single bee. Then, as times improved, a supper was appended, and the five-pail kettle pot-pie became an institution. This was especially so at the mowing-bees. Twenty to 25 scythes was a common field force; and all these in full clip, all in stroke, laying their well-mown swaths right round the meadow, with the boys and spectators, whetters and the bottle-tender—altogether an exhibition as, in these machinery times, will never more be witnessed.
>
> At one of these mowing-bee suppers at the widow John Sowles' the table was set the whole length of the ample

kitchen, the pot-pie was steaming on the servers, the weary but genial-hearted mowers seated themselves around the generous board, until every place was filled. Peter McMillen, who had bossed the field, coming in and running his eye along the lines, stepped directly in front of the fireplace, and taking Jim Mott, a great, green, grown-up sixteen year old field spectator, by the shoulders, just keeled him backward over the bench . . . and very coolly seated himself instead—Mott meekly making his exit, amid the convulsed roar of laughter of the entire company.

There were also "bees for plowing—planting bees, hoeing bees, and then the never-to-be-forgotten husking bees, with its story-tellers and song singers." There were even manure-hauling bees—for men only, when barns had to be cleaned—while woman had their own special bees.

Whether you call it a bee or not, this custom of working and then eating together persisted into the era of mechanization, being rechristened "changing works." In 1858, Holden Kelley, of Pawlet, had a group of neighbors helping him cut and stack oats in preparation for a threshing bee. At noon, all the workers repaired to the house, eager for dinner—to find, arranged in the sun before the house, a row of kettles and a frying pan of salt pork. There, Hannah Kelley explained to her husband, was the men's dinner. There was, she reminded him as she had already many times, no wood of a size for the kitchen stove and she had, for the last time, struggled to split some of those huge chunks designed for the living room stove. So now he must make the best of it. She'd done her part. The hungry, but amused neighbors, well aware of Holden's reputation for deferring such tasks, had already seized axes and a crosscut saw and were on their way, some to cut down birches from the grove across the road and others to split those parlor-stove chunks. In time, they had a bountiful dinner, though lacking the pie usually provided on such occasions. Blackberries and cream had to serve for dessert. In any case, Holden Kelley's woodshed was never again empty of kitchen firewood. A bee could, thus, become an instrument for exercising social pressure as well as for getting needed work done enjoyably.

Warning Out

If, however, there appeared in a town a new resident whose nonactivities suggested that he might in time become a burden on the community, the townsmen forestalled that emergency by warning him out. Chapin Keith arrived in Barre in 1801 from Uxbridge (Massachusetts) "with his young family and was duly warned out of town, lest he should become a charge on the good people of Barre. It was a custom of the time, if any came that it was doubtful about." Chapin Keith, it was to turn out, was a man of unusual gifts—becoming a judge of the probate court and a high sheriff, an office he held for many years.

Other towns shared the same cautious habit. Of Cabot, it was written:

> If a family came to town that had been duly "warned out," the town was not obligated to assist them; but if not, the town was liable. A very uncharitable record to put down for all our early towns; if we could not add, it was usually about as serious a matter as appointing a hog ward, to which office every man in town married during the year, even the minister, was candidate at the next town meeting. The old settlers were fond of practical jokes and received them very complacently. I have seen the record where the warning out went so far every family in town was warned out.

The following warrant is copied from the old records of Dummerston and shows the kind of instructions then issued to the constables by the selectmen:

> State of Vermont Windham County Dummerston Apr. ye 2d, 1781. To either of the Constables in the Town of Dummerston Greeting: In the Name and behalf of the freemen and by the authority of the same we command you forthwith to Warn all the tranchent Persons that is not Inhabitants of this Town that have not been in the Town one year from this date that is liable to be a Town Charge to Depart forthwith out of the Town with their Families if any they have.
>
> . . . To the authorities there must be some visible means of support, something external in the appearance of the newcomer, or he must leave within a year from his time of advent. If he had "but a thousand a year" known only to himself, he must go according to the warning. Good habits, honesty, uprightness, and educational accomplishments would not qualify a man for citizenship.

In accordance with the order issued on April 2d, 1781, about fifteen families were warned out, the warnings issued on April 14 and 18. Of course they didn't leave immediately; some never did.

"Very little is now remembered in regard to the condition of these families warned out of town that year," a historian wrote during the

1880s, "except that of Joseph and Jemima (Stoddard) Bemis. Mr. Bemis was about 24 years old, had one child at that time and had served through the Revolutionary war. He must have been all right physically. He did not 'depart immediately' but remained to earn a living without 'town charge,' bring up a family of 6 children, and pay for a good farm."

Some of Winter's Special Problems

All over Vermont, winters could be harsh but nearly always harshest in the northeast, where none of the tempering influence of Lake Champlain's waters could be felt. It was a Caledonia County resident who told of having nine months of winter and three of late fall every year. Coventry, somewhat farther to the north, had "as late as April 14, 1829 . . . snow 4 feet deep on a level in the woods"—a not altogether unusual occurrence.

> In Granby, a Mr. Bell who was trying to establish a home has told that he worked hard to break a road two miles from his house towards Guildhall for two entire days. In the winter of 1816, I think it was, when the roads were blocked up with snow, his bread stuff failed, and he started with a bushel of wheat on a horse to go to Guildhall (some 12 miles distant) leaving a family of small children alone with their mother, and one or two of them so sick that he hardly expected to find them alive when he should get home; and after wallowing about two miles through snow drifts, had to turn his horse back, put on his snowshoes and take his grain on his back and go his gloomy way to the mill.

When the compassionate miller had ground Mr. Bell's grain to flour, he sent his hired man back with Bell, now thoroughly exhausted, to help him home with his heavy burden. There, gratefully, he found his family well.

Mr. Bell had good reason for expecting the worst. Already, "in the December previous, Mr. Bell's mother, a woman in the prime of life, started from Guildhall for Granby one very cold morning on horseback. The next morning her horse was found in the barnyard and the woman in the road, within one hundred yards of home, dead. Apparently chilled too much to sit upon a horse, she fell or got off and after crawling a rod or so on her knees, sunk down in despair on her bed of snow."

In Morristown, halfway across the state, a man by the curious name of Comfort Olds, having lost one of his oxen, borrowed a pair to go to mill (about 12 miles) with, expecting to be back about the middle of the week, but a severe snowstorm prevented. Thinking he had (at home) only wood enough to last a few days, he must return and leave the team. On Wednesday night, though late, he arrived at his home. Mrs. Olds had sat up late, waiting for him, till she had burnt up all the wood she had, and went to bed with her two little children . . . After a while he came to the door and called to come in. At first she did not know his voice, but supposed somebody had come to tell her Mr. Olds had perished in the storm . . . He cut wood enough to make a fire to get warm by. Next morning he got wood to last through the remainder of the week, and started back to Cambridge to get his team, and on Saturday he arrived home with the grist.

So close to disaster did those early settlers live!

Winter or summer, there was one constantly recurring crisis that the father of a family had to learn to deal with. Either he himself mastered the art of midwifery or, whatever the weather, went forth to fetch home a midwife who might remain at his home to assist the new mother as long as needed or until a greater emergency called her elsewhere. When, on April 13, 1774, young Israel Putnam Dana of Danville chose to arrive, his father—presumably having served as a soldier under General Putnam during the French and Indian Wars—"had to draw the midwife 6 miles over hills and through deep snows, on a hand-sled. So exhausting was the labor that, stopping to rest for a moment at the sugar camp of his neighbor, Obadiah Smith, he sunk down insensible, and Mr. Smith went on with the doctress; thus rendering an important service to his future son-in-law—the child then born—who twenty-four years after became the husband of Sarah Smith."

Hunting Game in Winter

The same winter weather which made life so risky and added to the labors of fetching midwife or doctor could also bring rewards to the plucky and lucky. Settlers needed the occasional lucky break for until they could harvest their first grain crops, and frequently thereafter as need for food demanded and opportunity for securing it offered, hunting was a source of meat and warm furs as well as leather for shoes, harnesses, and such.

Moose and deer hunting was also resorted to to supply the deficit of meat. The country north of this town [Burke, in Caledonia County] for many miles, at that time was an unbroken wilderness, where moose and deer were found in great numbers. It is the nature of these animals, in the winter season, to herd together in considerable numbers, especially when the snow is very deep, which circumstance greatly facilitates the means of taking them. The most hardy of the veteran settlers would resort thither on snow-shoes as soon as a sufficient depth of snow had fallen, and surprise and slay them, and after dressing them, select the best part of the flesh for food, and carry it on their backs a distance of 7 or 8 miles, through the wilderness to their homes.

Soon they were devising handsleds with runners five or six inches wide to slide easily, like skis, over the snows and make it possible to haul out loads up to 200 pounds instead of the back-packed 100 pounds.

Eighteen-Froze-to-Death

Eighteen sixteen, that year when there was no summer, fell hardest on marginal lands where men and their animals depended for survival on each year's crop.

During this year, the inhabitants of Hardwick suffered much from snow and frost. A heavy snow began to fall on the 7th of June and continued to fall until the 9th. The sheep had just been sheared and had to be covered again with their fleeces; but there was little hay for them or for the cattle, and many of them died. The forest leaves were all killed and the woods went in mourning through the summer.

Hiel Hollister described that same year in Pawlet, over 100 miles to the southwest of Hardwick:

But 1816, which is within our own remembrance, was the greatest year of famine . . . There were frosts every month of the year. Winter grain was a tolerable crop, but summer grain and grass were almost a total failure. There was scarcely a bushel of grain raised in town. There was great destitution and distress in the following winter and spring. Many cattle perished and many people were reduced to the last extremity. Benevolent people divided their scanty stores with the more destitute, but the selfish took advantage of the opportunity and put on exhorbitant prices.

Starving sheep and cattle were slaughtered and their lean flesh salted down to carry the people through the bleak winter ahead and until the next year's crops could, with luck, be harvested.

Eighteen sixteen was so bad in Worcester, a town nearly ten miles to the north of Montpelier, that nearly everyone left town, some never to return. The Brown family was, in fact, the only one left in town and Mr. Brown saw his opportunity and took advantage of it the next year:

> When Mr. Brown was left by all his neighbors in full possession of the town, he took advantage of the situation to improve his own pecuniary interests. He had at this time a few sheep, a yoke of oxen and three cows. Having the whole range of the cleared land on which to keep his stock, he went to Montpelier and hired four or five cows, for which he paid $4 per year each. He found a ready sale for all his butter among the families in Montpelier at 13 cents per pound and fed the (skim) milk to the hogs, raising pork for sale, and so prospered in his affairs, turning the misfortunes of his less enduring neighbors to his own benefit.

Incidentally, though the historian neglects to point this out, he was thus keeping the cleared land cleared against the neighbors' return. Cows love to browse on tender young bushes.

A couple of years later—in 1818 or 1819—Mr. Brown was on his way to visit Massachusetts to help settle his father-in-law's estate. In a New Hampshire inn he was asked where he came from. "Oh!" exclaimed one man, "I have heard of Worcester. I have heard that all the inhabitants of that town except Mr. Brown have left the place, and that he has thrown his family on the town."

"The story you have heard is true," said Mr. Brown. "My name is Brown and there is no other family living in town but my own."

His place being halfway between Montpelier and Elmore, "he had frequent applications from travellers for refreshments . . . he concluded to open a tavern . . . Travellers were entertained in this log tavern until 1824 or 25, when he built a large two-story house, the one now standing, for a tavern."

The Good Squire

Well remembered in 1881 by the oldest citizens of Dummerston, the year 1816 was known as "Poverty Year" or, more feelingly, "Eighteen-froze-to-death."

> The mean mercurial temperature that year was about 43°
> . . . The early frosts of September destroyed the unripe

corn, which some farmers vainly tried to save by early husking and spreading. Famine stared everyone in the face . . . About 15 miles up the river on the New Hampshire side, in Walpole, was a wealthy farmer, Thomas Bellows Esq., who had a good crop of corn. He had more than he needed for his own use, and what he had to spare was sold in small quantities at the price in years of plenty to such men as needed it for their families and could pay for it only in day's labor, and were obliged to carry it home in a bag on their backs. Speculators were hard hearted in those days, as now, and took advantage of the situation . . . to speculate in corn.

One such man called on the "Squire" to purchase corn and asked his price. He was much surprised to learn that it was no more than in years of plenty, and he said he would take the corn.

"How much would you like?" inquired Mr. Bellows.

"I will take all you have to spare," said the speculator.

"You cannot have it," stammered the Squire, for he had an impediment in his speech. "If you want a bushel for your family, you can have it at my price, but no man can buy of me to speculate in this year of scarcity."

Hearing of this years later, a visitor was moved to write the following poem:

> In the time of the sorrowful famine year
> When crops were scanty and bread was dear,
> The good Squire's fertile and sheltered farm
> In the valley nestled secure from harm:
>
> . . . .
> And buyers gathered with eager greed
> To speculate on the poor man's need;
> But the good Squire said, "It is all in vain;
> No one with money can buy my grain;
> But he who is hungry may come and take
> An ample store for the giver's sake."
>
> The good old man to his rest is gone,
> But his fame still shines in the golden corn,
> For every year in its ripening grain,
> The grand old story was told again.

Churches and Churchgoers

What kept settlers going through times of cruel adversity was the inner certainty that a Divine Being was watching over them. Religious forms varied considerably but even deist Ethan Allen, whose beliefs so shocked the more conventional, was firm in his reliance on a very personal God, though not expecting Him to be a substitute for a man's own initiative.

The Preachers

Soon after the settling commenced, ministers of the gospel might be seen traversing the woods and hunting up scattered sheep in the wilderness. They would ride on horseback, or go on foot, as they might be able, with no other equipage than a bridle, saddle, and a pair of saddle-bags containing a Bible, psalm-book, and a spare shirt or two, or, if on foot, with less baggage. Thus equipped, they would travel through the woods, mud, and snow, preaching at the doors of log houses, or in the forest, any where that was most convenient. And in some cases they have been overtaken in storms, lost their way and have lain out all night . . .

Things began to change once meeting houses were raised in the towns.

> The writer has seen a woman and her children riding an ox-sled in a deep snow, while the man walked by the side of his team, with a shovel in one hand and a shamgar weapon (ox-goad) in the other, going to meeting, with hay on his sled for his oxen to eat while he was worshipping and a chain to fasten them to a stump.

The preachers also changed. In Fairlee, on the Connecticut River, Reverend Nathan Miles, reputedly of "liberal education," had settled in 1779.

> It is said of him that upon a certain occasion, while preaching to his little flock, upon the Sabbath, in his own house, in the midst of a sermon his wife approached with a message . . . immediately thereupon, he remarked that "the service would be suspended for a few moments," and passed into an adjoining room, put on his hat and veil, passed out through the room in which the congregation was seated, and hived a swarm of bees, came back and commenced his discourse where he had left off, and went through his sermon.

If the Lord permitted bees to swarm on the Sabbath, He intended they should be hived that day. Moreover, Reverend Miles did not expect the Lord to take his minister's side against the stings of protesting bees.

Meeting Houses

"In those days," Amos Churchill of Hubbardton would recall, "all made it a point to attend church with their families, every Sabbath, preaching or no preaching." He further told, "After people began to build meetinghouses and to meet in them, there was no such thing as a stove thought of for warming them, for many years, except the women's foot stoves. It was encouraging both to minister and people in a cold day, to see a good supply of them come in well filled" (with live coals, of course).

The building of a new meeting house was a matter of prayer, planning, saving, and, frequently, of argument. In 1790, a close-communion Baptist Church was discussed in Randolph, and "it was suggested that it would be expedient to have it painted and a lightning rod put up to ensure its safety. Deacon Flint said he was willing to have it painted, as he wished the Lord's house to look as respectable as his own and he would assist in having it done, 'but,' said he, 'I will never give a cent for a lightning rod; for after we have built the Lord a house, if he chooses to set fire to it and burn it down, he can do it. I shall never object to his doing as he pleases with his own!'"

Support for Ministers

Ordained ministers were hard to secure—harder to support. In Thetford, minister "Dr. Burton labored more or less on his farm until age and infirmity prevented. His salary was never more than $283.33 and that was at first made payable in wheat and other products. With this small salary he was able to accumulate some property."

Similarly struggling in nearby Strafford, was Elder Aaron Buzwell with a large family of boys and girls to feed and clothe on the pittance provided by the church over which he presided. The story goes that

> Late one fall the Elder visiting at Judge H's found him slaughtering sheep, both the fat and the lean; and, inquiring why the latter were killed, was told that it was to save the expense of keeping those that were old and poor, or such as had got the scab, and would die before the winter was over, anyway; but if killed, then the pelts would be saved, and the carcasses given to the hogs.
>
> "That's a good idea," said the Elder, "and I must try it on a few in my flock." "Then, Elder, you really have some scabby ones in your flock?" said the Judge. "Yes," anwered the Elder, "but you have the advantage of me; I can't save their pelts."

Keeping the Sabbath

Travel on the Sabbath was then considered sacrilegious, and in no way to be permitted. From Poultney comes the story:

> One morning, as the people were assembled for worship, a little Scotchman was walking to the east, and as he appeared to be going past the meeting house, the tithingman stepped up to him, and demanded the reason of his travelling on the Sabbath. He replied that he was a minister and was on his way to preach in Middletown (8 miles). By this time, a number had gathered around him, being rather suspicious that it was a false pretense, and questioned him closely. Finally, as they were destitute of a

minister that day, they proposed to him to remain and preach to them. He consented . . . They were all well pleased with the sermon, and permitted him to go on and preach in Middletown that afternoon.

Did they, one wonders, help him go? Did someone, perhaps, lend him a horse? Most had arrived on foot or, if coming from a distance, on horseback in summer, in an ox-cart in winter. "In summer, the man, if he was the owner of a horse, rode to meeting with his wife seated on a pillion behind him, and a child seated on a pillow before her; and sometimes another and smaller child in the mother's lap, encircled by one of her arms."

Though the thrifty Scots who settled in Caledonia County had found the nearness of "a good Presbyterian meeting" decisive in their choice of places whereon to raise their homes, when the Sabbath arrived their thrifty souls might have to struggle with their consciences. Three Norris cousins, working on newly cleared lands, had such an issue decided for them in an altogether memorable way for, of course, here was a matter in which the Lord would have the last word.

In the spring of 1793, these cousins supplied themselves with provisions sufficient, as they supposed, to last through the spring's work, when they were expecting to return to Peacham for a while. They had no such thing as a team or even a hoe to work with; but with their axes they hewed out wooden hoe blades from maple chips, hardened them in the fire, and took saplings for handles. With these they hoed in on Nathaniel's ground two acres of wheat; but Saturday night came, when they had sowed only one acre and they found they had only provisions enough to last them one day longer . . . They had been trained to keep the Sabbath day. However, they now held a council, concluded that it was "a work of necessity," and hoed in the second and last acre on the Sabbath.

"We shall see," said Mark and David, "whether this acre will not yield as well as the other." Reaping time came; the proceeds of the two acres were stacked separately and the time for comparing drew near . . . The stack which came from the Sabbath day's work took fire from a clearing nearby, and every straw and kernel was burned.

To the Presbyterian consciences, the moral of the tale was all too clear.

Far from Caledonia County and a half-century later, a good Methodist decided to boil down his heavy run of sap on a Sunday.

While carrying his pail of syrup home, he stumbled and fell, thus pouring out upon the ground his whole day's yield. Never again, no matter how heavy the run of sap, could he be persuaded to boil on the Sabbath.

Even in Caledonia County, though, there were folk who could maintain perspective and occasionally humor on the subject of religion. Mrs. Francis Whipple, who came to Hardwick in 1804, had "a great fund of cheerfulness and was often very shrewd. A fanatical minister called and said, 'You sometimes entertain ministers?'

"'Yes, if they have a recommendation.'

"'And what would you say to one from Heaven?'

"'Go straight back, 'tis a poor country here for such a man.'"

Wild Neighbors—The Indians

An advantage that Vermont settlers had over New Hampshire neighbors was one that they only presently could appreciate. "The powerful and dreaded tribes of the Iroquois on Lake Champlain, and the Abenaquis . . . who ranged the Connecticut valley and the forests of Canada, each laid claim to the fair hunting grounds of northern Vermont, and this being border land between them, never became permanently settled." With no settled Indians to claim the lands they were clearing, people moving into Vermont, save near Lake Champlain or the Connecticut, would not be persecuted with torture and tomahawk.

Along the borders of Lake Champlain, however, and in the river valley, Indian episodes did occur, for the tribes would not easily forget the value the French had placed on settlers' scalps during the recently ended French and Indian Wars. Soon they were to find an equally remunerative market, during the Revolution, among Tories.

A grimly amusing tale from the river valley tells of a somewhat doubtful occurrence:

> During the war, several men were clearing land not far from Cow Hill. One morning, as they went for lunch in their camp, leaving axes behind, an Indian stole down from the hill—where also were two Tories—and counted and examined the axes and fled back. The Tories insisted on going down to scalp and massacre. "No," said the Indian, "we no meet men who use such big tomahawks. We want three Indians to fight one big white man. We no go." The Tories yielded and they went away.

Sheep-raising Bridport, along Lake Champlain, produced a more believable tale of an Indian raid:

> A party creeping stealthily up the bank toward the house were discovered by Mrs. Stone in season to throw some things which she knew they would be sure to carry off, if found, out of a back window and into the weeds, and, concealing some valuables in her bosom, sat down to carding before they came prowling in. The Indians, not satisfied with what they found on the premises, drew near Mrs. Stone, who had been sitting during this fearful visitation, with her children around her, carding all the while, apparently as unconcerned as though surrounded by friends, instead of Indians and thieves. One young savage, suspecting she had some things concealed about her person, attempted to run his hand into her bosom, whereupon she so dexterously cuffed him in the face with the teeth-side of

her card, he quickly recoiled from the invasion. Another young Indian flourished a tomahawk over her head; but an old Indian, struck with admiration at the coolness and bravery of the woman, laughing in derision at the defeat of his companion, ejaculated heartily, "Good squaw! Good squaw!" when he interfered and led off the predatory party, and Mrs. Stone kept quietly carding on, till quite sure they had made their departure.

Escape Artist

Some years earlier, in 1763, there came to Shoreham, not far from Bridport, a Paul Moore who, having run away to sea at the age of twelve and remained a sailor for twenty years, had taken up his grant. He was thriving though handicapped by a badly set broken ankle that had given him a permanent limp. When the war reached Shoreham,

A few soldiers, probably a scouting party, turned in to spend the night with Moore, who was keeping castle in his hut of logs alone. Soon they heard the fearful war whoops and the house was immediately surrounded by a large party of Indians. Moore and his party defended the premises until morning when the exultant enemy broke down the door and rushed in . . .

The Indians had previously burnt his mill, and saddled and bridled his horse, ready for departure; but after setting fire to the house, a dispute arose about their plunder . . . At night they encamped at Crown Point and guards were placed over the prisoners. Moore, who had feigned so much lameness that they had given him a ride upon his own horse most of the way, they did not take the precaution to bind. His weary guard fell asleep . . . Moore took his gun, blanket, and some Canada biscuit, and started for the lake . . . through a thick grove of young saplings. Bringing into practice his sailor habits, he made his way for some distance, by swinging from one sapling to another without touching the ground.

Reaching the lake, he found that, while there was snow on the ground, none remained on the ice and that there was a log on shore that reached out onto the ice. He crawled out on the log, put on his creepers, then jumped onto the glare ice,

leaving no tracks behind . . . At length he came to one of those cracks made by the change of temperature between day and night. He made marks upon the ice with his creepers, and then took them off, and followed down the creek until he arrived opposite the mark; he made other marks as if he had crossed there, and putting on his creepers again, walked off a gunshot distance and spread his blanket on the ice, upon which he lay down with his ready-loaded gun.

By morning, three Indians, though slowed by Moore's ruse, were catching up. The first one, believing Moore had safely jumped across the crack, leaped and fell into the icy waters to drown. Moore picked off the Indian's astonished companions and escaped.

Connecticut valley encounters with Indians were sometimes more gruesome, sometimes more heartening to people now aware there are two sides to any problem of human relationships.

Raids, Real and Imaginary

From Maidstone, in the Connecticut valley, comes the following doubtful tale (recounted in the 1860s):

> We had a visit yesterday from an aged lady, who told of a Mrs. Chipman whose husband was at work in the field and attacked by a party of Indians and his head split open . . . in the sight of his wife in the house, who took her three children and fled to the woods [but remained] in hearing of the house. One of the children was a very crying babe, which she put to breast, every moment expecting it would cry and discover her place of concealment.
>
> While thus hid under the trees and thick foliage, she could hear the Indians come to the house and imitate, as well as they could, her husband's voice—saying, "Come, Molly, the Indians gone. Come back, Molly, come." As she did not come, they went away and she and her children were saved.

Knowing her name and her husband's voice suggested they had known the family previously. What offense, real or imagined, were the Indians trying to avenge?

In October, 1780, there took place a Tory-Indian raid on Royalton, in which over twenty homes in that town were destroyed with neighboring towns suffering to a lesser degree. Settlers who were not marched off as captives, to be sold in Canada, were left confronting the winter with starvation staring them in the face.

From Tunbridge, first settled in 1776 or thereabouts, comes the most circumstantial account:

Just before the light of morning on the 16th, a merciless body of 300 bloodthirsty Indians broke in upon this quiet settlement . . . with the most fiendish yells, and [the inhabitants] were suddenly awakened to the fearful realities of savage captivity . . . With barbarous cruelty the Indians destroyed almost everything valuable; nearly every barn with the contents they burned, furniture broken, bedclothing thrown into the flames, feathers torn from the ticks, thrown into the air, and set on fire, the odor of which spread over hill and vale . . .

This horde of Indians had left Canada intending to destroy Newbury. Their chief commander was a British lieutenant . . . their pilot a villain by the name of Hamilton, whom the Americans took a prisoner . . . in 1777. He had been at Newbury and Royalton on parole of honor, escaped, went directly to the enemy, and was doubtless the instigator of these awful depredations.

They now proceeded to the house of Mr. Elias Curtis . . . Mrs. Curtis had just awaked from her slumbers . . . and was about dressing herself as she sat up in bed, when the savage monsters entered the door.—One of them instantly flew at her with a long knife in his hand and seized her by the neck; but while in the very attitude of inflicting the fatal wound, discovered a string of gold beads around her neck which attracted his cupidity and averted the dreadful stroke. Instead of taking her life he simply cut the string to secure the glittering beads, but quick as thought, she snatched the string from his hand, and with a jerk scattered the beads on the floor. Struck with surprise and pleased with her bravery and coolness, he now only good humoredly exclaimed "Good Squaw! Good Squaw!" and . . . left her to gather up her golden treasures.

In 1868, those beads were still in the possession of her descendants. At that time, her daughter Polly, aged seventy-seven, corroborated the story.

River Crossing

Whether the party that raided Royalton and vicinity in the center of Vermont were on their way to or from Connecticut River settlements is not quite clear. Just when raiding Indians reached Bradford on the river is a question:

In the autumn of 1780, when the Capt. [Robert Hunkins] was at home again, a scouting party came in, saying that the Indians and Tories were coming in strong force, and would be there before morning. There was, of course, great alarm, and immediate efforts were made to get the women and children across the river to Haverhill [New Hampshire]. A foggy and dark evening was upon them. The men were resolved to stay and defend the place. Their only means at hand for taking their families across the river were dug-out canoes and but few of them. Capt. Hunkins hastily constructed a raft of boards, and while taking over his first load of passengers, his wife, with his infant son in her arms, was left with others waiting anxiously for his return. At the second passage she, with so many others came on the raft that it was overloaded; and before they could get over, was found in the utmost danger of sinking. The Captain asked the man assisting him if he could, alone, bring the raft to shore if it were lightened. He thought he could.

"Then, Sister Eaton," said he [Captain Hunkins], "you and I must take our chance in the river!"

She knew that he was a strong swimmer and trusted in him for help. The case was urgent; no time for deliberation.—He plunged into the water—she, like a brave woman, as she was, quickly followed him. Their feet could touch no bottom. He, acting with great self-possession and energy, succeeded not only in keeping her head above water, but in bringing her to the desired shore . . .

The enemy were really coming, as had been expected; but learning that the men of Newbury had been fore-warned and were ready for them, went off in some other direction to plunder, burn, seize captives . . . wherever they could.

From Newbury there also comes a very perceptive analysis of the Indians' point of view:

The first settlers . . . found the Little Ox Box and the Great Ox Bow, both cleared intervale—the hills so swarded over and a tall wild grass so abundant, the cattle found sufficient fodder. The Indians dwelt on these same meadows for a time with the settlers. They had bitterly felt this encroachment upon their rights, in these beautiful and favorite grounds . . . It was a fine country for them. It was a fine country to cultivate and suited to their imperfect means. The soil was rich, the river abounded in salmon and the streams in trout, and the whole country was plentifully supplied with game—bear, moose, fowls.

It was the half-way resting place between the Canadas and the shores of the Atlantic; and while this was retained, it was the key that opened the door to or shut it against the most direct communication between the colonies and the Canadas; and what was more than all to the Indians, it was their fathers' sepulchre.

Joe and Molly

An Indian named Joe appears frequently in early accounts, all of which suggested that he was accepted and liked by his white neighbors and that the feeling was mutual: "Old Joe had no passion for war himself, but he was a great whig and rejoiced in the defeat of the British whom he could never forgive the slaughter and dispersion of his tribe in Nova Scotia . . . After the War, some St. Francis Indians came down to persuade him to return with them to Canada, but, so deeprooted was his hatred of the English and English authority, it was in vain." Because of this, "he had taken his resolution to never set his foot on their soil." Even when hunting a moose that failed to respect the international boundary, Joe stuck to his vow. "He quit the pursuit, saying facetiously, 'Good Bye, Mr. Moose.'"

Joe's wife, Molly, gained considerable eminence among the settlers as a doctress and nurse. In a fight,

Norris fell, or was knocked into a great fire . . . hair and clothes were scorched, but the main injury was in one hand which was badly burned . . . Molly Orcutt was known as an Indian doctress, and then resided some miles off near the lake (Memphremagog). She was sent for and came and built her camp nearby and undertook the case, and the hand was restored . . . Molly's fame as a doctress was now raised. The dysentery broke out with violence that winter, particularly among children, and Molly's services were again solicited, and she again undertook the work of mercy, and again succeeded . . . Molly retained the nature of her prescription to herself, she prepared her nostrum in her own camp, and brought it in a coffee pot to her patients.

No pleas or offers of reward could persuade her to reveal the secret of her medicine .

In the following March, however,

as Mr. Joseph Elkins and his wife were returning from Peacham, they met Molly . . .; she was on her way across the wilderness to the Connecticut river, where she said she had a daughter married to a white man. Mr. Elkins inquired into her means of prosecuting so long a journey through the forests and snows of winter, and found she was but scantily supplied with provisions, having nothing but a little bread. Mr. Elkins immediately cut a slice of pork of 5 or 6 pounds out of the barrel he was carrying and gave it to her. My informant [Mrs. Elkins, apparently] remarks that she never saw a more grateful creature than Molly was on receiving this gift. "Now you have been so good to me," she exclaimed, "I will tell you how I cured the folks this winter of the dysentery." and told him her receipt. It was nothing more than a decoction of the inner bark of the spruce.

From the symptoms and the cure it seems that the illness had been scurvy—particularly the infantile form, which may suggest dysentery. Over two decades earlier, Captain James Cook's men, landing on our western coast, had cured themselves of scurvy by the use of "spruce beer." Winter diets of the settlers were notably low in the needed Vitamin C.

In any case, Molly had earned herself a sort of immortality, for today in the Danville area we may find flowing out of "Joe's Pond" a stream labeled "Molly's Brook" which passes through "Molly's Pond" before reaching the Winooski River. Both Molly and Joe survived to advanced age, Joe outliving Molly, to be taken care of by a local family and to receive from the state of Vermont a pension of $70. He was the last of the Indians in that area.

In Guildhall on the Connecticut River about 60 miles north of Newbury, the Stockwells lived in peace with their Indian neighbors, who often crossed the river from New Hampshire to visit the Stockwells, though never with hostile intent:

Many times has Mrs. Stockwell, on dark and rainy nights, on hearing the Indian whoop, gone alone, with her firebrand for a light, and taken the canoe over and brought the savages to her house. Their house was a general resort for the Indians, with whom Mr. Stockwell traded, purchasing their furs and giving various articles in return; but his authority, or that of Mrs. S. they never disputed—the tapping of his toe on the floor being sufficient to quiet them when most rude or riotous.

The Animals

Historical accounts from all over Vermont mention a variety of wild animals—catamounts, wolves, moose, deer, beavers, lynx, sable, and, of course, bears. One settler insisted that "bears were the only wild animals that troubled the settlers. They destroyed their crops and stock, and gave great annoyance."

Other settlers would not have agreed altogether. From Sheldon, in the northwest corner of the state, comes a statement:

> Wolves, in particular, were a great annoyance for a long time. Whole flocks of sheep were sometimes destroyed by them in a single night. Fires had to be kindled about the barns, and lights hung in the yards to frighten them away . . . So bold were they, in some instances, that prints of their paws have been found upon the snow-covered windowsills in the morning.

Catamount

An occasional encounter with a catamount—panther—is also recorded. Abel Smith, going from Eden to Hyde Park, a distance of nine or so miles, for a load of hay

> came near being attacked by a panther . . . Previous to starting, his wife cooked a piece of pork which . . . was put in a sack and thrown on the load. After reaching Hyde Park and obtaining his hay, he started to return; the snow was deep, the travelling tedious; night came upon him and found him far from home. Becoming faint and weary from hard walking and long fasting, he thought he would mount his load and partake of his lunch. Nearly as soon as he had done so, his dog, who was naturally a very resolute creature, gave a low growl and jumped upon the load. Mr. Smith endeavored to drive him off, but the more he tried, the closer did the dog crouch to him. His oxen also partook of the fright, and soon Mr. Smith, to use his own words, heard a scream which made his hair stand on end.
>
> Knowing the character of the enemy with whom he had to deal, he hurled his piece of meat, which he had just removed from the sack, as far back in the road as he could and seizing a large bough which grew over the road . . . succeeded in wrenching it off. Armed with this weapon, he started his cattle into a run . . . the panther meantime screaming terriffically. But when the panther reached the meat, he stopped to devour it. Accomplishing this, however, he renewed the pursuit, but had fallen so far in the rear, that after giving a few screams to denote his disapprobation of the means used to cheat him of his prey, he gave up the chase.

Treed by Four Bears

The above adventures took place during winter when the animals were, obviously, having as lean a time as the settlers. Bear adventures, however, are recorded for all other seasons when bears were not hibernating. The Marsh children encountered their bear along the Waterbury River in spring. It must also have been spring when Mr. Cutler practically stepped on a family of cubs.

> Mr. Cutler, the first settler of "Woodford City," on one occasion lost himself in the woods, and wandered around until sundown. Seeing no prospect of getting out that night, he began looking around for a place to lodge and, stepping over an old log, found himself in a nest of young cubs. The little bruins immediately gave a loud alarm which was answered by the old bear about ten rods distant. Mr. C., entirely without weapons, made for the nearest tree with all possible dispatch. This was a beech, its nearest branch about 20 feet from the ground. He sprang up and barely got his feet out of reach, when she struck at him with her paw. Finding his chance was good for staying through the night, he ascended into the branches beyond her reach and cut off some small limbs and fastened himself to the tree with withes. Mrs. Bruin kept near the foot of the tree in close watch until after daylight, when she took her family and moved off to other quarters.

Whereupon Mr. C., having had a chance to survey the land from his high perch, descended the tree and took his way homeward.

A Bear-Back Ride

> The 1896 history of Danby tells of Solomon Reed who has always been a tough, hard laboring man, and a great hunter . . . Capital stories are told of his encounters with bears, even during the last few years.
>
> One of those which happened about thirty years ago is worthy of notice: Solomon, together with his brother Ichabad, who was a young man of feeble health, was out one day in what is known as "Fir Swamp" after balsam. This swamp is situated nearly to the top of the mountain, and was some considerable distance from the house. They had been there but a short time when the dog, which had followed them, commenced barking at a short distance from them, near a sort of cave or den in the rocks, which signified that there was something in there.

Believing it to be nothing more than a coon which the dog had tracked down, Solomon thought he would venture in. So laying his gun down by the mouth of the cave, he crawled in to see what was there. He soon discovered that it was a bear, and called upon Ichabad to hand him the gun . . . Taking as good an aim as possible by the light of her eyes, he fired, but the contents (powder) failed to take effect. Bruin, not liking such an unceremonious call, immediately rushed out through the passage, which, not being very spacious, gave Solomon considerable of a squeezing.

The bear, upon coming out, at once made an attack upon Ichabad, who stood at the mouth of the cave. The dog immediately closed in for a fight, and acted as if Bruin had been as rough and unceremonious as his master had been, in intruding himself upon her notice. Solomon, on hurrying out, saw at a glance that his brother must have help immediately, and commenced an attack upon the bear, which drew her attention from Ichabad. The dog and the bear then became engaged, and Solomon seeing that the dog would get the worst of the fight unless he had help, stepped astride of the bear and took an ear in each hand.

When she felt the whole weight of this new element in the controversy, which was made to bear upon her, she turned her attention from the plaintive and suppliant tones of the dog to the more defiant antagonist on her back. The dog having found there was fighting to be done, now applied himself vigorously to the bear's haunches, whereupon she commenced descending the mountain, Solomon maintaining a firm hold on her back, while Ichabad continued to beat the bear with the breach of his gun.

The dog's mode of fighting soon had the tendency to lacerate her feelings so severely that she now turned her special attention to him, having no further fear of the men. Thus the dog would fight until seeing he would get the worst of it, Solomon would step astride of the bear, while his brother kept plying his blows, drawing her attention from the dog, first being under, then top, for the distance of a mile or more down the mountain, by which time the gun had been used up around her, and she was completely exhausted . . . Solomon and the dog was then left to contend with the bear, while Ichabad went for another gun, and the bear was then soon killed. Solomon was not much injured by the adventure, but his brother never fully recovered from its effects.

The Three Bears

In September, 1766, Mrs. Strong, who had come to Addison County from Salisbury, Connecticut, the previous February to settle on her family's grant, had a bear adventure slightly reminiscent of Goldilocks':

> Mrs. Strong, whilst her husband and a few neighbors had joined together and gone . . . to Albany to procure necessaries for the settlement, one evening was sitting by the fire with her children about her . . . The kettle of samp intended for supper had just been taken from the fire, when, hearing a noise, she looked toward the door, and saw the blanket that served the purpose of one, raised up, and an old bear protruding her head into the room. The sight of the fire caused her to dodge back. Mrs. Strong caught the baby, and sending the older children to the loft, she followed and drew the ladder after her.
>
> . . . the bear, after reconnoitring the place several times, came in with her cubs. They first upset the milk that had been placed on the table for supper. The old bear then made a dash for the pudding pot, and thrusting in her head, swallowed a large mouthful and filled her mouth with another before she found it was boiling hot. Giving a furious growl, she struck the pot with her paw, upsetting and breaking it. She then set herself up on end, endeavoring to poke the pudding from her mouth, whining and growling all the time. This was so ludicrous, the cubs sitting up on end, one on each side, and wondering what ailed their mother, that it drew a loud laugh from the children above. This seemed to excite the anger of the beast more than ever, and with a roar she rushed for the place where they had escaped aloft . . . and now commenced a struggle; the bear to get up, the mother and children to keep her down. After many fruitless attempts, the bear gave it up, and towards morning moved off.
>
> After Strong's return, a door made from the slabs split from basswood and hung on wooden hinges gave them more security from like inroads in the future.

Boating Bear

Sometimes it was the bear who, turning tables on humans, came out ahead, as Mr. Strong himself was to learn:

> At another time, Strong and Smalley were crossing the lake . . . in a canoe and when near Sandy Point, they saw

something swimming in the water . . . As they drew near . . . they found, instead of a deer, it was an enormous black bear that they were pursuing . . . a consultation was held. They had nothing but an axe, but they had too much pluck to back out . . . Smalley brought the boat up in good style and Strong, with all the force of a man used to felling the giants of the forest, struck the bear full on the head. The bear minded it no more than it had been a walking stick instead of an axe, but instantly turning, placed both paws on the side of the boat, and upset it, turning both men into the lake. The bear crawled up onto the bottom of the boat, and took possession, quietly seating himself, and looking on with great gravity whilst the men were floundering in the water. Smalley, who was not a very good swimmer, seeing the bear so quiet, thought he might hold on by one end of the boat, until it should float ashore; but no, Bruin would have none of their company; and they were obliged, each with an oar under his arms to sustain him, to make the best of their way to Sandy Point.

The sight of the bear serenely floating off on the bottom of their overturned boat was not soon to be forgotten by the struggling men who eventually located the boat, empty of contents and bear, on the shore some distance from Sandy Point.

The Doctor's Wild Ride

Even funnier than the boating bear is a tale that comes from Brookfield, some 13 miles south of Barre on the Second Branch of the White River:

On one occasion, a physician was summoned in the night from the hill to visit a man on the Branch. He started on horseback and while descending the hill was alarmed at a cry behind him which he took to be that of a catamount. He quickened his speed, the animal, as he supposed, being in hot pursuit. The bridge across the stream had that day been removed for repairs except the string pieces, but it being dark, the man dashed on, ignorant of the peril, having known nothing of the removal of the bridge. Arriving at the first house, he sprang from his horse, remarking that the devil might have the horse, if he would let him (the physician) alone. Being questioned as to his route, he replied that he had crossed the bridge, which the other denied as impossible. Both went in the morning to the bank of the stream, where tracks of the horse were found across the string piece to the opposite side . . . the animal that scared the doctor . . . proved to be an innocent screech owl.

As soon as those basic requirements of living—a shelter and food—had been met, settlers were bound to look around for ways to improve their standard of living. Usually this meant devising ways to make money or the equivalent—to barter products of the land for services or vice versa. Fortunate hunters might have furs to sell or knowing eyes might have perceived mineral resources which eager hands might exploit. More often it was just the hope of some such windfall that kept hungry settlers going from one harvest season to the next. Often small profits from a necessary local industry supplied the wherewithal to purchase items not otherwise available, and sometimes cash might come from less-than-legal sources.

For the original proprietors, few of whom actually settled on their grants, the item of first importance was to make sure that settlement took place, or else they ran the risk of having an unsettled grant declared null and void. A typical grant, that of St. Johnsbury, dated August, 1770, specified:

> That some or one of the grantees should within three years next after date, settle on the tract granted, so many families as should amount to one family for every 1,000 acres of land—or plant or effectively cultivate at the end of three years, at least 3 acres for every 50 acres of land granted capable of cultivation .

also that no one should

> by their Privity, consent or Procurement, fell, cut down, or destroy any Pine Trees suitable for the Royal Navy. Otherwise the Grant should be void and the land revert to and be vested in the grantors.

To escape such a threatened reversion, various methods were tried to encourage settlement. In June, 1763, the proprietors of Arlington (some 11 miles to the north of Bennington) had met and duly voted "to give a bounty to the first ten settlers that settle in town in one year," the amount of the bounty ranging at ten shilling intervals from six pounds down to one pound ten shillings. By May, 1764, the same proprietors, aware of the importance of a mill in attracting settlers, were voting to "give fifty acres of land to any man who will set up the first Grist Mill on a stream east from Simon Burton's dwelling house and about one hundred rods distant, if said mill be up and fit to grind by the first day of November, 1765."

Not surprisingly, the man who won that fifty-acre bonus was Remember Baker. The other settlers in that town profited equally. To get ahead, they needed power beyond that which their own muscles might achieve, and where was power to come from save wind or water? Where there was no appreciable fall of water, as in Alburg, close to the northern part of Lake Champlain, wind would be tried, there being built "a wind-mill for flouring on the west shore of the town, about 3 miles from the Province Line. This was quite a relief to the inhabitants as the nearest mills were from 10 to 25 miles distant, and across the water."

Steam as a motive force, though already tried in a few special machines, would not be used to turn mills for a long time. For most settlers there remained only the power supplied by falling water, and that meant a brook with a reliable flow throughout the year, if such could be found conveniently near.

Water Power

Brookside property was highly valued, for every settlement needed a mill close enough so grain could be hauled to it, ground, and then hauled back home on the same day. The settlers often had to settle for less. Early residents of Brunswick (near the Connecticut River and about 20 miles south of the Canadian border) had "no mills either for the manufacture of lumber, or converting their grain into meal and flour, nearer than Haverhill, New Hampshire, a distance of 65 miles." It would have been a very long 65 miles when there were no roads, few carts, and much of the hauling had to be done on manback.

A settler who had raised a crop of grain had to find a way to grind it before he could use it himself. He might use a plumping mill that prepared corn, one meal at a time, or he could take a large sack of grain to a gristmill, if he knew where to find one. Some of these were crude, like the one set up by Joseph Ball on Hall's Brook in Concord, in 1795, some 40 miles farther south than Brunswick though still on the Connecticut River. This was described as a "rough specimen"— so much so that "a Mr. Powers having got some grain ground there, his wife, as he said, 'tried to sift it with a meal sieve, but could not, it being so coarse. She next tried to sift it by using a ladder for a sieve, but it wouldn't go through between the rounds, and it was only by taking out every other round that the thing could be accomplished.'"

In western Vermont, also near the Canadian border, Joseph Beeman and his eldest son were arriving on foot from Bennington in 1786, carrying all their supplies and tools on their backs. Manpower, unassisted by any mechanical device, cleared the land and rolled up a cabin that the whole Beeman family would call home the next year. Somehow they found means to prepare the salts of lye, so valuable for barter, to plant turnips and a small quantity of corn and, with these harvested, all tightened their belts for a winter during which the cow must exist on "turnips and browse."

Maple Sugar

In spring, the Beemans were able to earn themselves a bit of income by making "maple sugar to the amount of 300 to 400 pounds . . . The utensils were troughs dug out of basswood for catching the sap and a three- and a five-pail kettle for boiling. The boiling utensils for Captain Broadstreet Spafford were a tea-kettle, a frying-pan, and a porridge-pot." Naturally, all the family shared the work of sugaring.

A self-styled progressive businessman of our day who had failed to acquaint himself with the facts of sap flow was once heard to remark that Vermonters were a shiftless lot to work at sugar making only in the spring. Of course, the fact is that there are only a few weeks during the spring when maple trees can be tapped and every sugar maker exults in those years whose weather patterns permit a longer-than-usual flow. Today he gathers his sap in numberless buckets, each hung on a spout he has inserted into a tree, or connects those spouts to a maze of plastic pipes which deliver the sap to a centrally placed tank (sap holder). In a large shallow oblong evaporator, it is boiled down to about one-thirtieth of its original volume. This is syrup. Sugar requires yet further boiling down.

In times when a metal pail was a precious rarity and plastic unheard of, the collecting and boiling of sap and the storing of its products was a problem, described from Fayston, though it could have been duplicated anywhere in Vermont:

How did our settlers live? In every department of labor almost nothing to do with. For making of maple sugar, the first five-pail kettle owned in town, Caleb Pitkin (1773-1813) brought it from Montpelier (about 15 miles) on his back, and sap troughs had to be made (by hollowing logs), and the sugar house was two huge logs with a kettle hung between, the smoke and ashes inclined to blow towards you, the sap had to be gathered by hand, and where was the man who owned a sap holder? When sugar was made, where was it to be stored? James Pitkin told the writer how his father (Caleb) provided for this emergency. In June, he peeled birchbark, soaked it, and sewed it with a strong wax-end, and this made a large box, less the bottom, but (next sugaring season) he sat this on a smooth piece of bark, with a sap trough underneath to catch the molasses (i.e. syrup that oozed out of the sugar) and he recollects many times eating biscuit and butter very near the sap trough. The box, he thought, would hold 200 pounds (of sugar).

When sugar houses came to be built and a long evaporator installed over a stone or brick "arch," sugar maker Moses Holden of Middlesex invented a device—a sap-feeder—to keep just the right amount of sap constantly flowing into the evaporator so that he need not be on hand every second watching the boiling. This device worked on the same principles as the floating contrivance which controls the amount of water running into a flume. Made by a local tinsmith, it was still in use in 1882, four years after its inventor's death.

Maple sugar was important as a local food and as a medium of barter. In 1790, 40 families in a single town produced some 13,000 pounds. The 1870 census showed that a town of about 1300 population was producing nearly 54,000 pounds, plus 1200 gallons of syrup, per year.

The Mills

Everyone wanted some labor-saving devices and machinery. Machinery meant wheels and wheels had to be powered by water flowing over millwheels. One of the earliest mills was for fulling, cleansing, and thickening woolens by wetting and beating, using lye soap made from potash.

By 1806, young Joseph Beeman, who had come north with his father twenty years before, had built a "mill for grinding . . . He also built a saw-mill." The year 1791 saw the first mill at the Great Falls of the Lamoille River, also both a grist and sawmill. Previous to this the inhabitants had gone to Burlington, about 12 miles, or Vergennes, 22 miles farther, for milling. The first clothing works had been carried off by a freshet in 1830. A carding mill, built near the same site in 1828, was powered through an overshot wheel 26 1/2 feet in diameter, with water carried to it in a canal 75 feet long at a height of 35 feet above and across the road. In 1850 a planing mill was added near the falls.

Disasters like that during the 1830 freshet were all too common. By the late 1860s the town of Georgia had had "7 different grist-mills, 10 saw-mills, 6 carding and fulling-mills" plus one mill to press the linseed oil from flaxseed, 4 tanneries, 2 wagon shops, and a lime kiln. In 1871, there were "at present 2 grist-mills, one of which is in-operative most of the time for want of water, and the other a part of the time—2 saw-mills; and one shop where wagons are repaired."

Ice, as well as shortage of water, could add to a miller's problems.

> A Mr. Fullington, who runs the mill, left his home in the morning, and came through the woods to the mill; while engaged in cutting the ice from the wheel so that it might start the saw, the wheel started unexpectedly and drew him under and held him there, while the water poured upon him its pitiless flood of cold, for several hours, when he was providentially found and rescued alive, and lived many years to tell the story of the saw-mill.

Incidentally, in those days tree trunks were sawed into planks not by whirling circular saws but by straight-bladed up-and-down saws whose marks on the backs of furniture are sometimes used to distinguish the real antique from the false.

Blacksmiths

Mr. Fullington was doing only what all millers expected to do. When things failed to run they had to find out what was wrong and try to fix it. If the trouble was a damaged or broken metal part, they had to turn to local blacksmiths. Every town had to have at least one smith. Horses and oxen had to be shod and special caulks inserted in their shoes when snow and ice made the roads hazardous. Beyond that, a smith might be called upon to make or repair any article of iron. If his shop stood near the banks of a stream he might take advantage of the extra power available, as did Calvin Harmon of Coventry, who about the year 1823 "built a blacksmith's shop on the river bank a little below the falls and furnished with a trip-hammer—a hammer designed to be raised and lowered by water power. Jonas Coulting was the first occupant of the shop. The business of a blacksmith was much more laborious, as well as broader in its scope, than it is now." In the 1870s "his stock consisted mainly of . . . bar iron, 3 or 4 inches wide and this he had to split, hammer and draw into shape for all purposes, even to the making of horse-shoe nails. He was expected to make any iron article which was wanted, and he did make axes, hoes, edge-tools, hand-irons, shovels, tongs, and many other iron articles each of which is now regarded as a distinct trade. Samuel Cobb even made darning needles."

A blacksmith who could make a serviceable darning needle had to have as much brain as brawn. Edge tools and farming implements as well as darning needles had to be tempered, and in the judgment and knowledge of just how each kind should be tempered lay a blacksmith's greatest skill. Not every smith who could shoe a horse could make an axe that would survive the hard use of clearing away great forest trees.

Bartering

Neither miller nor blacksmith expected—though he might hope—to be paid in hard cash. There were so few coins in circulation then that some folk could barely recall when they had seen coins, let alone held any in their hands. What they did have, unless accident deprived them of it, was their strength and their willingness to apply it to needed tasks. Purchases were made by barter which usually included services in the arrangement. The Coventry historian described a situation that might have occurred in any Vermont town of the early days: "On one occasion when two bridges were to be built, the town voted 'that the inhabitants turn out voluntarily to build the bridge at Burroughs mill and that $45 be raised to build the bridge across the Black river, payable in labor at 67 cents per day . . . or in grain the first of January next." The first of January next was an accepted date for the settling of debts.

After pointing out that in a remote village like Coventry, transportation costs added materially to the prices folk had to pay, the writer gave a fascinating description of the process of paying up:

> Another circumstance which increased prices was that goods were sold mainly on credit, and for barter pay. The almost invariable terms were that payment should be made in produce in the January following the purchases, which, if the customer failed to do, he was required to pay cash and interest within the succeeding year. January was always a busy month with the merchant. All the teams in the vicinity were put in requisition to carry produce to market,

and when ten, fifteen or twenty two-horse teams were loaded and started for Portland, the merchant took stage or private conveyance, and reached that city in season to sell the loads and make his purchases so that on arrival of the teams they might be immediately loaded for the return trip

—a long and cold one. Should Portland have failed to offer satisfactory prices, the merchant sent his teams on to Boston. When, at long last, the railroad line extended into northern Vermont, Portland declined as Boston became the marketplace of choice, and prices in Coventry began to drop. The whole system, of course, was based on the integrity of both settlers and merchants.

Once there was some kind of road built, direct teaming to Boston from Cabot was done by Robert Lance:

> His team was 2 yoke of oxen; freight—salts, whisky, pork, and it took from 4 to 6 weeks to make the round trip. He usually made two trips a year . . . In 1838, Allen Perry began to run a six-horse team to Boston, regular trips, the round trip taking 3 weeks. The freight tariff was $20 per ton, his expenses about $50 a trip. When he came in with his big covered wagon, it was quite an event for the place. He run his team until 1846, when the railroad got so near, he sold his team and went to farming.

Lumber and Other Products of the Land

Settlers tried one small industry after another—tanneries, saddleries, and wood-working shops which produced not only cabinet-work but carriages and sleighs. A town's skilled blacksmith might, between stints at the routine shoeing of horses and oxen, turn bog iron or the iron from hematite ore into useful articles like fire irons, door hinges and latches, and, of course, nails. But the truly large-scale business of the early days was, besides the sale of ashes, the shipping of lumber to a lumber-hungry European market. Burlington, on Lake Champlain, was an early shipping port.

In 1797,

> It was a great undertaking in those days to go into the woods in the fall and winter and to cut and draw the masts, hew the square timber, get the deal logs to the mill and in the spring saw the deals and collect it all into one great raft and get it to market. The principal place at which the lumber was collected was at Winooski Falls; there it was rafted and the men with their tents, provisions, and

cookery utensils on board, started their long and tedious journey to Quebec.

These men not only went into the woods themselves to get out lumber and take it to Quebec, but they bought large quantities of others who did business in the vicinity on a smaller scale—men who in addition to their agricultural labors, would get out what lumber they could but not enough to form a raft, thus a large portion of the people were directly interested in the lumber trade.

The first rafts went via the Sorel River until the Champlain Canal opened in 1820. Rafting continued until about 1835, when lumber was loaded directly on boats. Inevitably, choice Vermont lumber grew scarce. By 1850, railroads were hauling Canadian lumber to ports and the free-wheeling days of the rafters became a dim memory.

On the eastern side of Vermont, Bradford had the Connecticut River to carry its lumber to market. The historian of that town wrote:

When this town was settled there was a heavy growth of pine trees in the eastern part. Many of them grew on the tract of land owned by Col. Barron; and I have been informed by some of the aged people that, after the close of the Revolutionary War, he and Gen. Morey entered into a contract with three Frenchmen, to deliver to them in the Connecticut River, opposite to Barron's home, 100 masts,

with, no doubt, a due proportion of smaller timber for yards and booms, for the royal Navy of France; to be floated down the river to Middletown, where they were to be put on board of ships, and transported to that country. Pine trees were then plenty and money scarce. Sticks of timber 60 feet long, were estimated by their average diameter, at the rate of 25 cents an inch. According to this rule, a mast 60 feet long and 30 inches in diameter would come to but $7 and a half . . .

These great trunks of trees were brought, by numerous men and strong teams, to the high bank of the river, near Barron's residence; and on set occasions, of which due notice was given, there would be a great gathering not only of men, but of women and children, to witness the log-rolling. To see these heavy logs roll rapidly down the steep declivity and dash into the river, throwing it into violent agitation, was not a little exciting.

. . . it was with the early settlers a great business to get their trunks into the river to be floated down and sold for ship timber, or to be converted into boards and shingles for building houses. The building of flat-bottomed boats for the conveyance of prepared lumber to market, and to bring up salt, rum, molasses, iron and other heavy articles of merchandise in return, was early undertaken and continued for many years. To descend the river was comparatively easy; but return, forcing the boat along against the current with oars and pike poles was hard work. To go in this way from Bradford to Hartford, Ct., a distance of some 200 miles, was a labor of some 4 or 5 weeks,

and involved getting through swift water and around the falls at Brattleboro and Bellows Falls, through canals.

Swift-Water Men

From Vernon, on the river at the Massachusetts border, comes a fuller description of the way boats were taken up the river past the rapids:

A large portion of the merchandise and productions of the eastern part of the State were formerly transported in flat-bottomed boats upon the Connecticut river from Hartford, Conn., to the northern part of Vermont. Their capacity for many years was from 10-20 tons. [Later boats could take 30-40 tons each.] Three men would take the boat from Hartford to the foot of swift water . . . then it required 10 extra men to take the boat the next ten miles over swift water. These swift-water men were a hardy, energetic, jolly set of men, ready at a moment's warning . . . They used white ash setting-poles, with a heavy spike in one end, and when there was a strong south wind, they could sail a large part of the way. At "Brattleboro tunnel" [a canal?] they drew the boat with a windlass, and at Leavitt's Rock with oxen . . . When the wind was favorable, they could make two trips a day to Brattleboro.

The first river steamboat appeared in 1827. These were "intended to tow the flat boats where the water was not too swift, and they would take along three at once." Inevitably, these threatened an end to the need for the swift-water men's skills. Steamboat traffic, in turn, heard its death knell when, in 1849, the first railroad engine and cars appeared in a river town.

Livestock

To members of an agricultural community, livestock was bound to be an important source of income, as well as a means of supplying their families with animal products, like milk and wool and, when an animal had to be slaughtered, meat and leather—the latter very important for shoes and harnesses. Wool, though, was destined to attain the widest importance, since merino sheep from Vermont farms would provide breeding stock to as far-flung areas of the world as Argentina and Australia.

Sheep

Hiel Hollister, of Pawlet, wrote, "Our farmers, for many years only kept a supply for their domestic wants . . . selling off yearly a few surplus grass-fed wethers. Before 1812, there were but few, if any, fine-wooled sheep in town."

An elderly Hubbardton farmer, reminiscing at about the same time as Hollister, agreed that a farmer at first kept only as many sheep

as would produce enough wool to clothe his family with their winter garments, or as much as the women could work up . . . As the danger from wolves grew less, sheep increased . . . but there was not enough [cloth] to supply the [store] demand until the Legislature took up the subject to encourage the growth of wool. Sheep had never been taxed; and about the year 1810 or so, the Legislature passed an act, freeing each man's poll [tax] from the list, who had that year sheared 30 sheep. From that time, sheep began to multiply.

The Napoleonic wars and Colonel Humphries of Connecticut helped that trend along. Fine-wooled merino sheep were rapidly being converted into mutton by the Napoleonic armies that had been overrunning Spain. The distressed colonel managed to arrange for purchase of some merinos in the Spanish Extremadura and to import them into the States. By 1812, both breeding and further importations had made possible the spread of the breed throughout New England. Breeding stock from these fine-wooled sheep would presently bring high prices, a fine ram selling for several thousand dollars.

Horses and Cattle

Horses and cattle, of course, were also a source of income, and one which Captain Stephen Davis of the town of Georgia well knew how to exploit. In 1786, he and his family

> came by way of Skenesborough, now Whitehall [N.Y.], and down the lake on the ice. Tradition says that there was a "drove" of horses and cattle, and that all were very fine animals, and in very fine condition. Capt. Davis and his sons after him practiced letting cows, oxen and sheep, to be returned with increase, or for a rental payable in labor; and in this way not only aided many beginners in making and stocking their farms, but were enabled to control sufficient labor to make more extensive improvements on their own farms, than any other of the settlers.
>
> They planted extensive orchards and sold immense quantities of apples and cider . . . Capt. Davis was respected in town, and elected to office on several occasions; but he never overcame his intense objection to paying taxes . . . At one time, aided by his son, Stephen jr., armed with pitchforks, he defeated the collector in an attempt to seize property for taxes. The collector procured more assistance, and made a second attempt. When it became apparent that he would succeed, Capt. Davis announced his determination to go to jail—an alternative which the law at that time permitted the delinquent to choose—rather than have his property taken. Georgia was then in Chittenden County, and the collector got up his team to carry him to Burlington, to jail.
>
> Meantime he (Capt. Davis) put on his overcoat, and

seated himself in a chair from which he would not rise. The collector, equal to the emergency, procured help and loaded him, chair and all, into the sleigh and took him to Burlington. On his arrival there, his numerous acquaintances flocked around him (Capt. Davis); and, for the first time in his life, he was persuaded to recant. He gave his note for the amount of the tax and costs and came back with the collector. Of course he paid the note on his arrival home, for that was a debt of honor—and no man was more scrupulously exact, when his word was given.

Liquid Assets

Vermonters presently were to become aware that they had, within the limits of their state, a potential source of income that depended only upon the whims of nature. To exploit it to the full would require a growing sophistication in the ways of "foreigners," as folk from outside the state long were labeled.

Vermonters themselves had been exploiting, in an altogether modest and unspectacular way, the medicinal properties of a variety of mineral springs discovered all over the state. The tourist-income potential took a bit more time to become evident. The middle 1800s were a time when such springs were attracting people in all parts of the world, promising them at one and the same time diversion and cures for an infinite variety of human ills. European watering places were legion and patronized by the best and most moneyed citizens. In America, Saratoga was becoming famous.

The Vermont poet, John Godfrey Saxe, described it all in 1868 in his "Song of Saratoga," which might have been the song of half a dozen, at least, Vermont towns:

> Pray what do they do at the Springs?
> The question is easy to ask;
> But to answer it fully, my dear,
> Were rather a serious task
>
> . . . .
> Imprimis, my darling, they drink
> The waters so sparkling and clear;
> Though the flavor is none of the best,
> And the odor exceedingly queer;
> But the fluid is mingled, you know,
> With wholesome medicinal things,
> So they drink and they drink, and they drink,
> And that's what they do at the Springs.

Writing in the early 1860s, the Vermont state geologist stated that several Vermont mineral springs were already considered "valuable for medicinal purposes . . . the number of those sojourning at the watering places in Vermont is annually increasing. Clarendon, Highgate, Alburgh, Williamstown and Newbury, are fast becoming the resort of those in quest of health or pleasure during the warm weather of summer."

Long a witness to a once thriving business that, like Saratoga, offered strangers a canny combination of medicinal waters and summer sports was the handsome sprawling old hotel of Clarendon Springs which, even when falling into decay, looked impressive:

> These springs were doubtless among the first ever visited for their medicinal virtues, and are probably more resorted to [in 1861] than any other in the state.
>
> Tradition informs us that their medicinal character was first discovered in 1776 by one Asa Smith, who resided in the eastern part of the town. He is reported to have "dreamed" of a spring in the western part of the town, and, full of faith, started through the wilderness and over the high hill that separates the two portions of the town, in search of the spring that would furnish water that should restore him to health. Arriving at this spot, he recognized it as the one he had seen in his dream, and accordingly at once drank of the water, and bound clay saturated with it

upon his swollen and inflamed limbs. The scrofulous humor which for years had been a source of continual annoyance, at once yielded to the potent influence of the water, and the man was soon restored to perfect health.

The state geologist cautiously ends with, "We do not vouch for the truth of this marvellous tale, but tell it as it was told to us."

Alburgh Springs, practically on the Canadian border, was a place of resort since 1816 . . .being very efficacious in the cure of all forms of cutaneous and scrofulous disease. The number of visitors to these springs has since gradually increased . . .

In 1834, the Mansion House hotel was built . . . a spacious hotel . . . with frontage of eighty feet on two streets and a piazza of two stories, and is built for the comfortable accommodation of nearly one hundred guests.

The Inns

Vermont inns had come a long way in the less-than-forty years since Nathan Robinson, Esquire, set one up in Stowe:

It was built of logs, 40 feet by 20, one story, floor made of split logs adzed off a little at each edge and laid split side up. There were two rooms, one a kitchen with one bed in it, the other "the square room," was supplied with three beds. There were three beds "above," a place reached by climbing a ladder, where one might lie in bed and trace the constellations at leisure. This house was warmed by an immense stone fireplace, which would take wood around six feet in length, not only giving warmth and comfort to all the household, including travellers and company, but also affording a most brilliant and cheerful light, at night, around which the family circle were wont to gather, including the guests and not infrequently most of the neighbors, who came in to hear the news from the older towns, and to while away the long winter evenings with jokes and songs and anecdotes of olden times.

Everywhere, fireplaces had become prodigious structures. The historian of a town somewhat to the north of Stowe, where there seems to have been a brick kiln, told:

Seven thousand brick were none too many to put into a chimney in which there was a fireplace 8 or 10 feet wide and of proportionate depth. The fireplace was a marvellous storeplace of light and heat. The back-log was part of the solid butt of a tree, which, with the fore-stick and top-stick of nearly or quite the same size, constituted the main structure for a fire. To this were added as many smaller sticks as the state of the weather required, and a few pine knots and other kindlings being thrust under and between the several logs, the whole mass was easily set on fire, and the flame went roaring up the chimney . . . One such fire lasted 24 hours, and sometimes several hours longer.

Wood was then, remember, "an incumbrance to be got rid of by any and all possible means."

A less pretentious and obviously far more crowded inn than Esquire Robinson's was established in Coventry in 1823:

Knights built a small house which was for some time the only dwelling on the hill. It served as a house of entertainment for such as came to examine land before purchasing, and a boarding house for settlers until they could build for themselves . . . his house was sometimes crowded to the utmost. It was inhabited several times by 23 persons, 8 of whom were married couples, with 14 children under 7 years of age. This little building which contained so large a population is now fifty years later one of Mr. Cleveland's out-houses.

Quite a contrast, in any case, with that "comfortable accommodation of nearly one hundred guests" at the Mansion House in Alburgh Springs scarcely more than a decade after Knights built his house in Coventry!

The Alburgh Springs hotel was designed as a profit-making venture and not for the struggling settlers trying to establish themselves and families. It was catering to citizens from other states who could afford the cost of treating ills, real or fancied, at the Springs. So successful was this venture for Vermonters only a generation or so away from the settlers that, by 1854, they were building the Missisiquoi House. "A new and commodious hotel," 124 feet in length and 40 in width, it also was for about 100 guests and boasted 3 stories with 2 piazzas of 2 stories. "From the Missisiquoi House as well as the Mansion House, carriages run to and from passenger trains on the Vermont and Canada Railroad, for the accommodation of travellers during the summer" who, in those preautomobile days, expected to stay put in such a hotel as long as their finances lasted.

"There are two springs . . . These springs are resorted to by pleasure seekers as well as invalids." Fishing, hunting, rowing, and sailing were some of the pleasures, but undoubtedly the greatest was the never-failing delight of sitting on one of those long, high-ceilinged piazzas, discussing with rocking-chair neighbors the foibles of all passersby.

In not-too-distant Highgate Springs the Franklin House was running lively competition, also accommodating about a hundred guests at a time. For its Champlain Spring, it was claimed that the "water has cured two cases of cancer, and consumption, scrofula, rheumatism, erysipelas, salt-rheum, and all forms of cutaneous eruptions—liver complaint, bowel complaint, & c., & c., and is especially a specific for dyspepsia, even in its worst forms."

If boarders found their ills failing to give way to those incredibly curative waters, they could always turn to a local physician, though whether they enjoyed his treatment could be another matter. In 1832 there was practicing in Highgate village a Doctor Bradley of whom it was written:

> From an anecdote of Dr. Bradley, we are led to conclude that he was a man of good, sound common sense. In his practice, it is said, he had a patient who imagined he was sick and sent for Dr. Bradley . . . the doctor came to the conclusion that there was no disease preying upon his system, and that it was purely in his imagination. He did not, however, inform his patient, who had been bedridden for nearly a year, of his conclusions, but told him there was a plant somewhere upon the east hills which, if he could find it, would surely cure him, and such was the hope and anxiety of the patient, he was prevailed upon to accompany the doctor in pursuit of it.
>
> The sequel is that they tramped all day over the hills, when the doctor was so much exhausted that he was obliged to give up the chase, while his patient seemed to be as fresh as ever and was from that day a well man, although they failed to find the desired herb.

Clearly, Dr. Bradley was a man highly skilled in the treatment of psychosomatic illness.

Trading with the Enemy

Livestock could produce hard cash for the men who had raised it only if it got to market, and like lumber most of northern Vermont livestock was sold in Canada. At least, it was openly sold there until the War of 1812 decreed that sales in Canada constituted illegal trading with the enemy. The war, though, could offer no alternate markets for the men residing so far from usual trade routes.

Men who were subduing the wilderness through the labors of their own hands and backs were not, though, of a kind to take too seriously a decree which insisted that yesterday's customers had changed from trading adversaries to fighting enemies. Necessity encouraged this feeling and also found interesting ways to circumvent the embargo. If the ways were not quite legal, neither—so many of the northern settlers were inclined to insist—was that accursed embargo imposed upon them by politicians who had comfortable homes in well-settled communities.

Disappearing Dead Livestock

The town of Franklin, within two miles of the Canadian border and closer to Montreal than to Burlington, would feel the pinch while car-

ing very little about maritime issues that were being decided in areas so remote in distance and in understanding.

> When the war of 1812 commenced, all market was stopped with Canada and the dwellers on the northern line of Vermont were deeply distressed. They really had no place of business. Troy, or Albany, N.Y., were too far away to be reached by teams, and little farm produce would pay to be carried so far in the winter, and in summer they had neither the time to go, nor much produce that would pay transportation. However some British subjects, neighbors and friends of those who dwelt in Vermont, sometimes appeared on the south side of the line, and left with their old friends sums of money, and soon after cattle, hogs, or horses were missing from their stalls, and nothing more was ever heard of them south of 45°.
>
> Mr. H. (Hon. Samuel Hubbard) had eight heavy hogs slaughtered in his corn barn, and one night they disappeared. He was at home, but made no search for them. Col. Fifield who was then in command of a regiment at Burlington, arrested and marched him between two files of soldiers with fixed bayonets to Burlington. He was thrown into the guardhouse, without fire, without a bed, and only a loose floor and poor rations, until some acquaintances told Col. F. he might expose himself to action of civil law for abuse of a prisoner. Comforts were then supplied him (Hubbard) and he wearied out 20 days in confinement, when he was marched back to Swanton for trial. As the colonel could not substantiate his charges, and feared the result of a civil suit for false imprisonment and abuse, he was glad to settle by paying $350. Further disturbances did not occur

but smuggling continued to thrive.

The Smugglers and the Law

While questions might be raised as to whether Mr. Hubbard's indifference to the disappearance of his pork truly constituted trading with the enemy, it was hard to doubt the intentions of other folk who were quick to turn a profit by trading in both directions.

> Dry goods, such as silks, muslins, prints & c. were deposited near the line often; and then packed on men's backs through the woods, by the custom-houses, and secreted until they could be transported by team or boat to the place of destination. The Troy and Albany merchants

often paid smugglers large sums for this service. Tea, sugar and tobacco, at different times, paid large profits as contraband articles . . . Pork could be bought in Plattsburg for one dollar per pound, the port of entry, or rather of prohibition, passed, they could go boldly into St. Johns (Canada) calling their loading "government stores;" and after disposing of it for two dollars per pound, load back with sugar, doubling on that . . .

The very next year, from the failure of the shipping to arrive in Montreal, tea paid just as high a profit to smuggle directly back. Frequent seizures, especially of potash progressing northward, were made about this time, and some 60 to 70 barrels had been stored in the locked barn on Windmill Point (Lake Champlain). A plan was concocted to relieve the customs officials of this and restore it to its owners [by removing siding boards when the officers' attention had been distracted]. Team after team sped northward over the ice-bound bosom of the Richelieu (River); and long before morning all had been deposited across the line in safety. My informant said, that he knew one team that got around so as to haul three loads and get in all right before daylight.

Smuggler's Notch, in Lamoille Country, with its cavelike recesses among piled-up rocks, was a favorite pass by which cattle could be headed for Canada "and in turn it was often used by the returning party bearing merchandise" which could be hidden among the rocks until it was safe to take it on and dispose of it profitably.

A man who was a boy of eight at the time of the War of 1812, would write rather cynically a half-century later:

Highgate being a border town, it is not strange that such a portion of the inhabitants as those whose loyalty was overpowered by avarice, should enlist in the smuggling enterprise. British gold and silver somehow found its way into the States and every substantial farmer had his old blue stocking leg filled with it. Every boy carried more or less . . . jingling in his pockets, and of course there was more or less smuggling and occasionally the smugglers got sore heads, but what of that, as they were getting prompt pay for the risk . . . Those engaged in smuggling were not so much enemies to their country as friends of gain.

There was another, kinder way of looking at the business. The son of Ephraim Adams, one of those four New Hampshire schoolteachers who took up neighboring grants in Franklin County, told it thus:

Our early settlers were much troubled for markets for their produce, depending upon Montreal attended with many annoyances, to say nothing of the occasional loss of a team or boat in the St. Lawrence River [especially when encountering thin ice] . . . When an embargo was laid on this market, as in the war of 1812, it is not to be wondered at (although all were loyal) that some so far winked at smuggling, as not to be of any great service to the government as witnesses, in enforcing the law against their neighbors . . . considerable droves of cattle were driven over our back roads and partly in the woods. We boys wondered why they had so many men—they often having a man to every six or eight head of cattle . . . so as to drive quietly and rapidly and be ready for any emergency.

A popular ditty of those days ran:

> There was old Sorrel Barber
> And also Silver Gray
> They swore they'd go a smuggling
> Until the Judgement day.

The Smuggler's Stratagem

Smuggling is a thriving business, even into our own day, at many international borders, and the tales produced by the business have an almost universal ring. One can find, for instance, on the Amazon or on the Brazil-Paraguay border, tales of adventures much like the one described for an adventurous soul of Scottish descent who throve during the War of 1812.

A resident of the border country described it all:

During the War of 1812, a pretty extensive business in the line of smuggling was carried on by some adventurous citizens of this and neighboring towns. Many droves of cattle were taken across the "lines," on which a good price was realized, and numerous loads of merchandise found their way "this side," notwithstanding soldiers were stationed along the border to prevent the illegal traffic.

This being the case, there must have been numerous exciting adventures between the United States officials and the "contraband dealers," some of which are still remembered, as related by the participators. The "smugglers' road," as it was termed, extended from some point on the Missisquoi River, in Sheldon, through this town on the east side of the pond, to the lines adjoining St. Armand, and the whole distance was then an entire wilderness.

William McKoy, a Scotchman, who came to this town from Clarendon, about the year 1800, was a shrewd, wide awake man and one just suited to this line of business, in which he took an active part, and as a consequence, participated in some novel adventures, one of which we will relate and style, *The Smuggler's Stratagem.*

At one time, preparations having been made to take a drove of cattle across the "lines," a certain night, and it being necessary to divert the attention of the Berkshire custom-house officer from the movement, McKoy undertook this part of the proceeding. During the day he persuaded the officer to accompany him to Franklin Center, for the ostensible purpose of intercepting the drove that was to pass, he said, on that side of the town. The officer was rather suspicious that all was not right; and as night came on, and no cattle made their appearance, he became uneasy and demurred at staying there, when the drove was probably passing on the other side. McKoy [said he] thought it would soon be along, when they would secure the prize, but after remaining as long as he thought necessary for the safety of his companions, he concluded he might be mistaken in the course taken and they had better correct the error at once. Proceeding with all haste to the north end of the pond, when they reached the "smugglers' road," McKoy, being a little ahead, plunged into the path, and riding a swift horse, was soon out of hearing in pursuit of his companions, leaving the out-witted officer in the forest, three miles from home, in the dead of night.

Another of the same man's stratagems—never to be duplicated on the Amazon—is also recounted:

McKoy was once arrested for debt on the "other side" of the line, taken to a tavern and placed under guard for safe keeping. Pretending to be in no way alarmed or disconcerted, he removed his hat, coat and boots, and seated himself by the fire, as it was winter and cold. Some men and boys getting up an excitement in the street, he asked permission to witness the scene. Not expecting any attempt to escape in his exposed condition, his request was granted. Watching his opportunity when the guard was not very vigilant, he took advantage of their remissness, and left. Taking a bee-line across the fields, and being in good condition to run, he distanced all pursuers, and escaped to "this side," freezing both feet in the race.

The law, whether of Canada or of the United States, was not always on the losing side. Officers, even when successful in interfering with smuggling, were inclined to be sympathetic with and understanding of their hard-pressed fellow countrymen, while conscientiously trying to perform their assigned duty.

> The Colonel (Clark), with a number of men, visited the township (St. Armand) . . . for the purpose of arresting a company of smugglers with a drove of cattle they had taken across the lines. The latter [smugglers, not cattle] supposing the former to be a British officer come to purchase their cattle, gathered around, eager for a good bargain, when, upon a given signal, part of the company were taken prisoner—the others succeeded in escaping. The confiscated cattle were now turned upon their back track, while the former owners were obliged to assist in driving. This they did so cleverly, that upon arriving in Sheldon, the Colonel having no further need of their services, allowed them to proceed to their homes. After the conclusion of the war, the smugglers were summoned to Rutland, to answer for their misdoings . . . upon counsel's raising a question of law, "that driving cattle on foot was not transporting beef"—and the point being carried—they were released.

The Black Snake

Smuggling was not always an amiable business, for it was bound to appeal to the avaricious, antisocial person who would not hesitate to kill if he thought he might get away with it. Such were the men who navigated the notorious smuggling boat, *The Black Snake*.

In the mid-eighteenth century, Britain's cloth-making establishments had so needed the potash used in treating woolen fabrics that they had foregone importation duties on potash from the colonies. During the embargo of 1808 and on through the War of 1812 only Canada was allowed to send ashes thus duty-free. However, it was extremely difficult to tell in England whether the trees that had produced a given batch of potash had grown to the north or the south of the U.S.-Canadian border. No dealer on this side of the ocean very much cared to make certain, as long as the trade continued to be profitable.

More than profitable, it was essential for most of the "hardy pioneers" to market their ashes if they were to survive.

It was fortunate . . . that pot-ashes, during all this time, brought a remunerating price in Montreal . . . Upon the sales of their pot and pearl ashes in Montreal, they depended almost entirely for the means of remittance to their creditors in American cities. So important was this traffic, that in most of the interior towns of Vermont, not a dollar in money could be raised, except by the sale of ashes . . .

Large quantities of ashes were brought to the ports of Lake Champlain, and sold at a small price to speculating smugglers who stood ready to purchase. This beautiful lake, with its secluded bays, shady nooks and uninhabited islands, offered a convenient highway to the smuggling boat, which moved only at night, and remained quiet by day . . .

The late Doct. Jabez Penniman, of Colchester, was collector of customs. A twelve-oared cutter, called the *Fly*, belonging to the custom-house department, cruised about the outlet of the Lake, and smuggling in that direction became uncertain and dangerous . . . The terrible *Black Snake*, with a crew of powerful and desperate men, thoroughly armed, had for months defied the government officials. Either by stealthily eluding their vigilance, or by overawing them by a display of hostile force, she had continued to freight large quantities of pot-ashes across the line to Canada. They (the officials) had at no time a force at their command sufficient to render prudent an attempt to seize the audacious craft.

Doctor John Stoddard, of St. Albans, a merchant and well-known smuggler, employed the *Black Snake* to transport ashes from St. Albans Bay into Canada . . . The boat had made several trips with complete success, but was at length encountered by officer Joseph Stannard, who commanded the crew (of the *Black Snake*) in the name of the United States, to surrender. Stoddard was on board, and persuaded the men to exert themselves at their oars. Stannard, being without force to back his demand, was compelled to witness their safe escape across the line into Canada. But the officers of the government were now fully determined upon her capture.

The *Black Snake* was built to run as a ferry between Charlotte, Vt. and Essex, N.Y. [across Lake Champlain to the south of Burlington and where a ferry is still running] and was used for some time for this purpose . . . She had a mast and one sail; was steered by a rudder, was never painted, but besmeared with tar, which gave her a black appearance.

John and Ezekiel Taylor, of Caldwell's Manor in Canada, purchased her to run as a smuggling boat; but when the trips became dangerous, they employed a man by the name of William Mudgett to navigate her. As she could carry nearly 100 barrels of pot-ashes, at a freight of 5 or 6 dollars per barrel, the enterprise was a paying one and justified some risk, nevertheless her audacious career was drawing to a close.

On August 1, 1808,

The *Black Snake* had crossed the line from Canada the previous night and had gone up the lake [carrying Captain Mudgett and a crew of six] . . . The men were to be paid by the Captain $8 to $10 per trip. Each man had a gun and they were provided with spike-poles to keep off the revenue boats—several clubs 3 feet in length—a basket of stones the size of a man's fist. They had, also, a large gun called a wall-piece or blunderbuss, the barrel of which was 8 feet and 2 inches long, and 1 1/4th inches in diameter in the bore which carried 15 bullets.

On coming from Canada they avowed their determination to fight their way back. They were not very well supplied with ammunition but had a jug containing 2 gallons of rum. Under cover of the night, they proceeded to Martin's Bay, on the eastern shore of North Hero, where they lay in seclusion through the day, and during the night went to the mouth of the Onion (Winooski) river [on the east shore of the lake] where they arrived at sun-rise. They kept on up the river, and reached a place called Joy's Landing, 3 miles or so from Burlington, about noon.

They drew their boat on shore some 60 rods above this. Mudgett ordered the men to clean and oil their guns, and to put in new flints where they were needed. He then proceeded in quest of provisions and ammunition, and returned with a supply toward evening. They shortly after this received tidings that the revenue boat was coming. Two men from Burlington, whose names are not given, came to the landing and informed the smugglers that they would not give the boat a load, as they were informed the revenue cutter was coming to take her . . . one of them said he would give the crew 10 gallons of rum if they would go down the river and take the revenue cutter.

. . . the *Fly* proceeded along the easterly shore of North Hero, after passing which, and when opposite Middle Hero, a man upon the shore waved his handkerchief. They came to, and were informed by him that the *Black Snake* had gone up the Onion River.

Having entered the river and being told where the smugglers' boat lay, the revenue men

> then rowed up the river, and, turning a small bend in the beach, came to the place where she lay; one end of her was on shore, fastened to some bushes. Mudgett stood on the beach a few feet from her, with a gun in his hand. He called to the revenue boat not to land; but they, disregarding his attempt to intimidate them, ran in immediately alongside, between the *Black Snake* and the shore.
>
> Mudgett retreated a few steps, but kept on threatening, and said, "Don't lay hands on that boat. I swear by God I will blow the first man's brains out who lays hands on her." Lieut. Farrington, who seems to have been a brave and prudent man, with several men then stepped on board the *Black Snake* . . . As the two boats were about to cast off, Mudgett came to the bank and cried to his men: "Come on, boys! Parade yourselves! You are all cowards! They are going to carry the boat off!" Ledgard (one of Mudgett's crew) came and called, in what was denominated, in the testimony given in the trial, a Methodist tone of voice: "Lieutenant, prepare to meet your God! Your blood shall be spilt before you get out of the river!"

A battle ensued in which three government men were killed (though not the lieutenant) and all the smugglers taken captive, to be put in a Burlington prison.

> The greatest excitement now prevailed throughout the entire region. The people were horrow-stricken at crimes like these, in the hitherto quiet and peaceable state of Vermont. They called upon the authorities of the State to maintain, inviolate, the dignity of the outraged law, and to let its tremendous penalties follow speedily and sure. The funeral of the three murdered men took place at the village of Burlington on Thursday, August 4th, 1808.
>
> The rancor of political feeling was greatly increased by the events which have been detailed. The annual State election being near at hand . . . a flaming handbill, headed by three coffins, was scattered over the State, and copied into the democratic papers [the Democrats, as contrasted with the Federalists, then being in power] in which "respectable federalists" were charged with attempting "to screen the assassins, and throw the whole

weight of guilt upon the government." . . . The authorities of the State acted with promptness and celerity. On Tuesday, Aug. 23rd, less than three weeks after the affray, the supreme court was convened in special session at Burlington

presided over by the writer, dramatist, and ex-suitor for the hand of President John Adams' daughter, Justice Royall Tyler.

In his charge to the grand jury, Chief Justice Royall Tyler alluded to the general dismay—"the agitation of the public mind that prevailed . . . that some were ready to condemn the accused unheard, while others, perhaps, were disposed to excuse, and if not to excuse to palliate." He said to the jury, that "if, in some moments of levity, any of you have thought that the primary laws of society, made for the preservation of human life, ought on this occasion to be relaxed, and to be accommodated to certain supposed exigencies of the times, purify yourselves from these prejudices."

In this mood, one crew member was tried, judged guilty of murder, condemned, and executed. The others, including Captain Mudgett, were tried some months later, convicted only of manslaughter and sent to state prison, where they arrived on June 1, 1809, "the second day after the prison was opened for the reception of prisoners."

Within a few years, when the embargo had grown up into war and smuggling become a way of life with some residents of northern Vermont, the prisoners were pardoned and soon disappeared altogether from the state. "Thus," wrote the historian nearly sixty years after, "closes the account of the career of these lawless and desperate men. No one of them is known to have regained, to any extent, the reputation lost by this blood crime. They removed either to Canada, or to distant portions of this country, and most, if not all, died as they deserved, in obscurity, neglect and poverty."

Liquid Contraband

One form of contraband, whose problems have persisted into our own century, was the liquid variety of a kind that had endowed the crew of the *Black Snake* with so much courage. Rum was then and had for long been a commonplace.

As early as 1793, the town of Tunbridge recorded "two very curious votes." "One was directing a committee to clear a spot for the meeting house by making a bee and to find rum at the town expense; the other, quite novel, 'Voted to raise the house at the expense of the town, only the committee were to find 2 barrels of rum out of meeting-house funds.' " The meeting house was not finished until 1797, but whether rum had a part in this delay was not noted.

In Coventry, a town within ten miles of the Canadian border and about halfway across the state from east to west, the 1820s saw two Harmon brothers giving land for a village common "on condition that the citizens should clear it of stumps and smooth the surface. They were slow in complying with the condition and, to expedite matters, it was agreed that whoever became 'the worse for liquor' should do pennance by digging out one stump. This proved to be much more effectual in clearing the land than in preventing drunkenness. A pint of rum afterward came to be regarded as a fair compensation for digging out a stump." Presumably the site was well cleared before 1825, when Lyman Beecher's stirring temperance sermons were published in book form and began to work on the minds and consciences of many citizens.

Of one St. Johnsbury resident, it had been told that "the old pioneer who was afterwards elected to the state assembly, used to make periodic visits to Barnet (about 10 miles to the south) and return with a two bushel bag of grain (around 100 pounds) on his back and a gallon of rum in his hand. Of course, the measurement of the latter was taken at Barnet." Presumably as the load grew heavier, the jug grew lighter.

Churchgoing citizens often shared that politician's predilection. In St. Albans the first full-time Congregational minister, Rev. Jonathan Nye, was installed in 1805:

It was not at once, however, that the Sabbath congregations presented the staid and orderly appearance common in older communites. Gen. Levi House, a lawyer of ability and one of the leading men in town, unfortunately became addicted to intemperance. In a state of partial intoxication, he, on a Sabbath day, decided to attend church and entered while Mr. Nye was proceeding with his sermon. He had not been long in his seat before he made an audible response to a rhetorical question propounded by the preacher. This was repeated, when Col. Seth Pomeroy, acting as tithing man [a man deputed to keep order during divine service] called out from the gallery, "Silence down there!" Gen. House, turning his glassy eye in the direction of the gallery, with maudlin voice exclaimed, "Silence up there!"

The passage of a century would not suffice to eliminate that kind of problem. An old-timer told an equally amusing tale of the town tippler of Pawlet, some 120 miles to the south of St. Albans. That tippler, equally drunk, also decided to attend church service and entered while the blood-and-thunder Methodist minister was holding forth. He—the tippler—started down the aisle and kept on while two ushers vainly tried to divert his path towards one of the pews. Finally, in a voice to match the preacher's, the tippler announced, "Behold! Here we come! Christ between two thieves!"

In the early days Pawlet boasted five distilleries, while Cabot, not so large and to the north of Montpelier, had twelve. And thereby hangs a tale:

> The cloud of war began to settle down over our country, and soon we were involved in a conflict with Great Britain, and Cabot distillers, only about 40 miles from the Canada line, lost no time in finding a market in that country for the product of their stills . . . obeying the divine injunction, "If thine enemy hunger, feed him; *if he thirst, give him drink!*" This command, so explicit in its terms, the towns situated near the border seemed bound to carry out; a large number of cattle were driven over, and no small quantity of whisky found ready sale among the British soldiery . . . It was smuggling and was rather risky business, but the commandment was plain, and imperative, and must be followed. And about this time, distilleries went into operation rapidly.

Ever since the first teller of tales invented the first fairy tale, people have been letting themselves be convinced that somewhere, out of sight yet reachable by determined souls willing to spare no effort, there lie treasures of one kind or another. In 1861, the situation was summarized by Mr. A. D. Hager, a scientific gentleman writing on "The Economical Geology of Vermont" (we'd call it simply "economic"). He wrote:

> There are those in the community who are ever ready to engage in enterprises that lead to the development of mineral wealth—indeed, it sometimes appears as if people were seized with a mania to dig for hidden treasures, whether it be in the form of "Kidd's money," "a splendid marble quarry," or a "valuable iron mine." There is scarcely a mountain peak in the State that has not in it some reputed hidden treasure: Old Lead Mine, Silver Mine, &c.—with a legend connected therewith, that years ago—but generally beyond the memory of the "oldest inhabitant"—an old Spaniard, Indian, or hunter used to go to replenish his stock of milled dollars, or to get lead for his bullets by cutting it off with his hatchet, and similar foolish and unreasonable declarations; and strange to say, all

these marvellous traditions have advocates and firm believers.

As a result of this crazed state of mind, there may frequently be seen deep pits, like wells, either dug in the ground or blasted out of solid rock; and in other cases, horizontal drifts are made in hills, resembling, in many cases, miniature railroad tunnels, at the end of which, it was anticipated, lay a fortune to all concerned; but instead of that, disappointment and loss were the result.

It is curious, yet painful, to observe with what tenacity a visionary schemer, who has supposed that a fortune was buried and in store for him, adheres to his preconceived opinions. No argument can convince him of his erroneous judgement: and approaching destitution and bankruptcy are, generally, the only potent influences that can induce him to desist and abandon his unprofitable undertaking.

Fruitless attempts have also been made in the State to obtain salt water and coal. If the amount of money expended in fruitless researches for coal, iron and the precious metals, were counted together, it would give a sum much larger than all the profits ever realized in the State by the working of metals.

Tiny bits of real gold have been found—the largest nugget reported by the 1860s having been valued at $14. Experienced gold prospectors, returning from California, tried panning for gold and soon decided the pursuit of native Vermont gold was not worth the effort. As for silver, the geologist tells us, "Notwithstanding the many reports of silver mines . . . we have never been able to learn the precise locality of even one workable mine of silver in the State." Of copper, however, there have been some profitably worked deposits until far outdistanced by those productive copper mines developed by Alexander Agassiz in Minnesota.

All in all, "For the habitual money digger, whose frenzy is engendered by the fortune teller, and who is lured on by 'mineral rods,' there is little hope of permanent cure, so long as he has the means to prosecute his wild schemes." The same, clearly, was to be said of gold and silver mines.

Vermont's Real Underground Treasure

When the geologist wrote of those frenzied diggers, he was not thinking of the real, if less spectacular, underground deposits. There was and is high-quality granite, for buildings or for gravestones. There are also materials for flagging stones, whetstones, and oilstones. There is roofing slate, soapstone, and limestone. The latter, when powdered, is spread on too-acid agricultural lands to improve fertility. Heated under proper conditions, limestone produces quicklime. Wrote the geologist:

> The uses to which quicklime is applied are many and varied. It is used to clarify the juice of sugar cane, and to generate heat and absorb the volatile gases in a compost heap; to purify the coal gas that illuminates our cities, and to bleach the rags of the paper-maker and the cotton and linen fabrics of the manufacturer; to render potash and soda caustic in the soap manufacture, and used in water to restore health to the invalid; to free the hide from hair in the tanner's vats, and when mixed with litharge to dye the gray whiskers of the bachelor; to stop the stench that might arise from the slaughterhouse, and to aid the chemist in his researches.

Today's uses may differ somewhat from those just listed, but quicklime is still an important product—and a valuable one, though not in the class of buried fortunes.

Of about the same chemical composition as limestone is the marble that occurs in the western areas of the state in many fascinating and valuable varieties. Only chips and waste marble would be converted into lime. As statuary, building blocks, and trim in a variety of places, marble continues to show its value. The first use of Vermont marble was confined to the gravestones, now blackened with lichen growth and roughened by nearly two centuries of weathering, that are still to be found in early cemeteries. The geologist wrote,

> Until 1804, marble was not sawed in New England, but quarries were selected where "sheets" could be split off, which afterwards were worked smooth to the desired shape with chisels in the hands of the workman. In the year A.D. 1804, Eben W. Judd, Esq., of Middlebury, adopted the plan of the marble workers who lived in the days of Pliny, and sawed the first marble in the State with a smooth strip of soft iron, with the help of sand and water.

A real and enduring treasure—Vermont marble.

Mines and Metals

The geologist assures us:

> The rocks of Vermont are too old to contain workable beds of coal—and were deposited long before the earth

was in a condition to sustain the luxuriant vegetation requisite for the production of the immense carboniferous deposits existing in the coal measures. But persons unacquainted with geology, and perhaps regarding the occurence of coal as accidental . . . have vainly sought for it . . . Disappointment must follow all such unwise ventures.

Lignite—so-called brown coal—has, however, been "found quite abundantly at Brandon . . . It is not found in beds, but in upright masses that extend down and cut obliquely through the beds of kaolin. There are two localities of it in Brandon, about sixty rods apart. The larger of these masses, situated contiguous to the ore bed of the 'Brandon Iron and Car Wheel Company,' having an area about twenty-five feet square, has been penetrated to a depth of eighty feet perpendicular, and the coal removed and used for fuel for driving the engine to drain the mine and raise the ore."

This brown coal, laid down at a "period comparatively not very remote," did not serve for smelting the iron ore. For this, huge areas of forest were cut down and converted to charcoal. By 1820, John Conant was erecting a furnace where

was cast the old "Conant Stove"—the first stove made in the State and a great invention for the time, and which was the wonder of the farmer's kitchen and sold in all the villages around and abroad . . . It was the first stove we ever saw and our father bought one and brought it home as a surprise. And never was anything brought into the house that created such an interest, it was the inauguration of a new era in the culinary kingdom. The pleasant fireplace with the swinging crane of well-filled pots and kettles, hearth-spiders with legs and bake-kettles and tin bakers to stand before the blazing logs and bake custard pies in—all went down at once and disappeared before that first stove, without so much as a passing struggle . . . The first Conant Cook Stove was made in the autumn of 1819 . . . the work of erecting a blast furnace in Brandon going on at the same time, and resulted in supplying a superior quality of iron for stove making . . . almost every variety of iron castings were made directly from the brown hematite ore of the region. The business proved a success and was prosecuted by Father & Sons for a period of 30 years and was the life of the town.

It was a great day when Brandon iron was used to mend a broken crankshaft for a fulling mill.

Bog iron was also to be had there, as well as beds of iron oxides—ochres—which supplied paint colors ranging from light yellow to dark brown as well as two shades of red. Geologist Hager wrote: "The extensive beds of ochre and kaolin belonging to the Brandon Kaolin and Paint Company cover an area of 80 acres." Kaolin "is used in the manufacture of vulcanized India rubber goods, and also in the manufacture of paper" and, of course, stoneware, earthenware, fire-bricks, and porcelain.

Yet another manufacture resulted from the availability of Brandon hematite:

> The manufacturing of scales was commenced in Brandon in 1857. In the early part of that year an arrangement was made between Mssrs. Strong and Ross, and the late John Howe, of Brandon, by which all the patents taken out by said Strong and Ross for improvements in weighing machines and platform scales, were assigned to the said John Howe, who was at that time engaged in the manufacture of pig iron and car wheels. Mr. Howe immediately commenced the manufacture of scales under the patent, retaining the services of both the inventors . . . In March, 1857, they manufactured for the Morris Canal Co. . . . a scale of 200 tons capacity, with a platform 70 feet long, one end being 7 feet higher than the other, which proved highly satisfactory to the purchasers.

By 1869, unfortunately, the Howe Scales Company went into bankruptcy as a result of "unfortunate management in the transaction of business." The company was revived after bankruptcy and is still a going concern, though now situated in Rutland, its ore no longer coming from Brandon mines. A by-product of Brandon mining operations during the last century was manganese ore, some being sold in Europe. Though the shrinking availability of metal resources has stimulated some talk of reviving old mines, such as the one in Brandon, in 1861 the state geologist looked upon many claims to mineral resources with a jaundiced eye.

> That noted personage, the "Old Indian," a myth that in days of yore visited so many lead and silver mines in the State, has also learned the location of several iron mines and confidentially imparted the fact to some pale-faced friend, but unfortunately the rocks and trees that marked the spots are generally removed so that the precise location is not now known. Numerous excavations, in different parts of the State, mark the spots where fruitless efforts were made to reach such hidden treasure by digging and blasting.

The Old Spaniard of Wallingford

The fascinating possibility of discovering a store of precious metal, already mined and, in some cases, converted into coin, is something to be rejected with reluctance, save by that geologist who reiterated that he had

never been able to learn the precise locality of even one workable mine of silver in the State. We did, however, find several excavations where *supposed* treasures were located, either in the form of silver ore, coined metal, or both. A case of the latter kind occurs in Wallingford in what are called the "white rocks," a precipitous range of quartz rock, situated about two miles east of North Wallingford village. At intervals, for the last twenty years [prior to 1861] companies of men have assembled here and worked laboriously in this hard rock, for weeks at a time, with the vain hope of finding a "cave" which some Spaniards had made in these rocks, a long time ago, by the removal of ore, and in which they had subsequently worked and reduced the ore to metal, and coined this into "Spanish dollars."

The story, briefly told, is about like this: When Richard Lawrence, of Chester, now an old man, was a boy, he did a slight favor to an aged stranger who was travelling through the town on horseback; whereupon he was told by the old man that for the kindess shown he should some day be richly paid. He informed the youth that he was a Spaniard, and that the saddle-bags upon his horse were filled with silver dollars that he had recently obtained from a cave in Wallingford. Many years before, when he was a boy, he and other Spaniards had come to this country, and discovered, in the mountains of Wallingford, a rich silver mine, which they had worked for a long time and very successfully. In order to keep the thing a secret, they had taken the precaution to smelt the ore and coin the metal, in the cavity made by the removal of the ore in the mountain. The mouth of the adit leading to this cavern was known to but few, and strict secrecy was enjoined.

After having worked several years and "made money enough," the party resolved to return to their native country. But here they were in a dilemma: They had an immense amount of money made, but no means for the transport of all of it. Pack horses were obtained, and bags full of the treasure were taken off and carried to Spain; yet large lots of silver in bars, and an immense amount of coined metal was left in the cavern, either to remain there forever, or to be taken by any of the party who should ever stand in need of any more money than that taken by them at this time.

Years rolled by, and this old Spaniard was the only survivor of that fortunate band of adventurers who had worked in the silver mine of Wallingford. He had left Spain to get another dividend from the treasury, and when young Lawrence met him he was upon his journey home, laden with the shining treasure. He was so favorably impressed with the prepossessing appearance of young Lawrence, that he finally concluded to unburden his heart, and, for the first time in his life, communicate to mortal man where this great treasure lay—with the condition that the young man should not tell of it while it was probable that the Old Spaniard should live; but *after his having a reasonable time to die,* the contents of the cave were all to be at Lawrence's disposal.

True to his trust, Lawrence did not communicate this intelligence to any one for many years, but finally told it confidentially to a few friends, and went to find the cavern. But alas! The adit leading to the subterranean storehouse of treasure could not be found.

After diligent search and fruitless attempts to find the opening in the side of the mountain of rock, it was concluded that the door had been closed by some great slide of rock from points further up the mountain. "Mineral rods" were procured, and a man found who could *work* (?) them, after which the location of the cave was pointed out. To reach it was a difficult task; but the immense wealth in store there would make all rich, and pay the expense of blasting to it, even if starting at the top of the mountain.

Money was raised, powder purchased, men employed, and the work of reaching the cave by blasting out the solid rock that lay above it was commenced and continued for several weeks, but finally abandoned for a time. Again and yet again the work has been resumed and abandoned. At times the mining party has consisted of more than a dozen men, who have vigorously pushed the work for weeks at a time. But, notwithstanding all these efforts, the hidden treasure is still unreached, and we are not permitted to record the discovery of that lost cave, or the remnant of that rich lode of silver.

We have given the foregoing account as we received it from those who owned "stock" in the mine. We give it not for sport, or to wound the feelings of any who engaged in the wild scheme, but merely as one of the many hundreds of similar examples where people are lured on and induced to dig for hidden treasures where there is no reasonable ground for supposing they have an existence.

The Old Spaniard of Essex

Against all the evidence of geology, a similar episode was reported from Essex, apparently some years prior to the Wallingford episode. Here again the old Spaniard makes his appearance—or the old Spaniard's uncle, perhaps. Here also, there is a new twist to the tale altogether in keeping with the fanciful nature of a treasure left by Spaniards at a time and in a locality where Spaniards would be most unlikely to visit, let alone remain long enough to discover buried treasure. Certainly, it should have been obvious that they would not be trekking from Canada with a heavy burden of treasure in a practically roadless wilderness. The obvious, though, is never obvious to folk who cherish their beliefs in fairy tales.

In 1824 and for several years following "no small stir" was made among that class of people in town most noted for their credulity and superstitious notions, by the assertion that, in a certain locality in the eastern part of the town, large quantities of gold and silver coin lay buried. The story runs thus: Many years previous to the settlement of this state a company of Spaniards came from Canada with a vast amount of silver and gold, and encamped on Camel's Hump, where they manufactured it into Spanish coin. Portions of this rich treasure were thought to have been buried from time to time along the route. In confirmation of this theory it was alleged that crucibles or vessels for melting the precious metals had been found near the Hump; that there were marked trees, extending from the latter place to Essex and thence northward toward Canada, evidently indicating the route taken by the rich Spaniards; and that an old Spaniard had died somewhere—who, as a dying bequest, divulged the secret to some confidential friend that a vast amount of money was buried in the town. Under such a combination of circumstances, who could entertain a doubt?

A few faithful friends, to whom the wonderful secret was communicated, were gathered together. Shovels, pick-axes and iron bars were brought into requisition, and under the lead of their juggling doctor who carried in his hat the mystical stone in which he could see the precise locality and enormous quantity of the concealed precious metals, or held nicely poised upon his forefinger the charmed stick which was certain to become mightily agitated and decline from its horizontal position at the presence of gold or silver, they went forth in "silence and in fear." With "lanterns dimly burning," they gathered around the spot indicated by the mystic stone and charmed stick and commenced the toils which were to be so soon rewarded with the sight of the precious coin. With all the energy of desperation and of fascination they labored on from day to day till at length their eyes were feasted with a sight of the hidden treasure.

But alas for poor human nature! The involuntary outburst of joy, as the goal of their ambition was now within their grasp, broke the charm, and the "chest of gold" disappeared forever from their view in the solid earth beneath. Several large holes in the vicinity remain [1868] as monuments to their credulity and folly.

The Man Who Corrupted Middletown

Such "monuments to credulity and folly" are also monuments to the desperate yearnings of essentially poor folk whose lives have been spent in backbreaking labors on the land. Perhaps, too, those monuments witness to the kind of human weakness Mark Twain laid a finger upon in *The Man Who Corrupted Hadleyburg*. In any case, the buried treasure reputed to be concealed somewhere in the township of Middletown, about fifteen miles to the southwest of Rutland, involved not only credulous townspeople, but a genuine imaginative con man and a group of suggestible, though sincere religious mystics.

The con man gave his name as Winchell. If there was another part to his name, no one in Middletown thought to record it. No one in that then remote little town knew exactly where he came from, though much later some were convinced that he was none other than the Wingate who was wanted on a counterfeiting charge across the state in Bradford, Vermont, on the Connecticut River. No one could say where he went when he disappeared as inexplicably as he had appeared—and that was exactly how he wanted it. What everyone agreed on was that while he resided in Middletown, strange things happened and that after his disappearance it was a long time before the sleepy little crossroads town reassumed its pristine character.

"Winchell," wrote the town historian who, during the 1850s, interviewed elderly citizens whose youth had been livened by tales of the fascinating, mysterious stranger, "turns up in Middletown at Ezekiel Perry's, in the fall or forepart of the winter of 1799. Here he staid all winter, keeping himself from the public eye." This matter of consciously avoiding the public eye was surely a bit of historical hindsight, since that "public eye" found little of interest in a small town composed of a central square with a lot of little dead-end roads winding up into the surrounding hills. On one of these roads was Ezekiel Perry's farm, rarely visited save by neighbors.

Anyone of our own day who has had dealings with a twentieth-century con man can ruefully recognize in Winchell a direct-line ancestor of the conner. There is the quiet, almost self-effacing manner, the virtuously shocked disapproval of the doings of questionable (though unacknowledged) rivals in his profession. This, of course, is accompanied by the earnestly expressed desire to become involved in something that should accrue to the advantage of the conned. Overriding everything else is that unrestrained imagination and a quick intuitive perception of exploitable human weaknesses.

By spring, 1800, Winchell, if a fugitive, was feeling himself relatively secure. He was also growing restless and, worse, bored with his situation as a "furriner" amongst men he considered dull yokels and who, he knew, regarded him rather doubtfully, as they did all furriners. To him, this formed an all-but-irresistible challenge.

As snow gave way to mud and mud began to dry a bit, Winchell would wander off into the woods which were showing their first faint tinges of green. There he soon recognized the witch hazel shrub, widely used in folk remedies and generally thought to be possessed of unusual powers. To a man of Winchell's temperament, unusual powers were not to be neglected. He cut himself some sticks "with two prongs in the form of a fork" and, "taking the two prongs, one in each hand and the other end from the body," began to develop his latent dowsing skills. First he worked by himself in the woods. Then, as spring progressed, he transferred his activities to Ezekiel Perry's yard, where his doings were not for long lost on his host or on neighbors and cronies of Ezekiel Perry.

The local yokels were dazzled. The town historian, writing some sixty years later when safely beyond the range of Winchell's persuasive personality, could take a more skeptical view of the rod: "Whether it is attracted by water or mineral substances in the earth, or moved by the imagination of the person holding it, is a matter for a philosopher, not for me. This much is quite certain, it was a very effectual implement with which to practice deception."

What was he doing with that stick? people who dropped by with increasing frequency would wonder and ask. He was, he assured them, doing nothing—and it was not a stick but a divining rod. The rod was doing it—showing where treasures might be buried.

Treasures! In Middletown?

"Why not?" he'd murmur vaguely while he continued to move across the ground. The rod twisted in his hand. Hm! Must be something metal nearby! Sure enough—there it was! An old ox-shoe, partially hidden by the mud that was closing over it. Not precious metal, but he couldn't expect that, not with a signal so weak.

Did he really mean, then, that his rod could reveal hidden treasure—real treasure? Now that, he murmured, was something they might test if they cared to undertake rather heavy work. He had, when in the woods, come upon a spot where his rod had twisted violently. No, he'd done nothing about digging there—too big an undertaking for one man.

Of course the men offered to do the work and Winchell, visibly moved, offered to share with them equally whatever treasure they might find. But there had to be conditions.

For one thing, all must swear to keep an absolute secret everything that had to do with the digging. That, all protested, they expected to do. Then Winchell, looking doubtful, "had recourse to his rod to determine whether they were sincere in their promises to keep the money digging a secret." The rod having reassured him on that point, he sallied forth, holding his rod before him while behind followed the men carrying picks and shovels. On a hill, "his rod fell or made some motion, which told him, as he said, that they had reached the spot where the precious metal was buried."

The now thoroughly excited men immediately commenced digging. "They worked hard for two or three days, and becoming weary, their enthusiasm began to cool and they began to show signs of giving out. Winchell held up his rod, got some motion from it, and told them the money was in an iron chest and covered with a large stone, and that they would soon come to it."

In that ground, a stone was a practical certainty, but the dazzled men, setting to with renewed vigor, were tremendously excited when they came upon one. Winchell then raised a restraining hand while yet again he consulted his rod, which told him that the men "must wait awhile before removing the stone or taking out the chest of money. It was now two or three o'clock in the afternoon and this man, the better to accomplish his purposes, kept his dupes away from the place until nearly sundown, when they were then provided with levers, handspikes and bars to remove the stone." Winchell, for his part, was comfortably provided with waning twilight. After again consulting his rod, he reassured them dramatically that there lay a great treasure almost within reach but that to put their hands on it, they must follow his instructions carefully. The men quickly agreed.

To begin with, he insisted, the time had come to divest themselves of whatever metal they might have in their pockets, so that nothing in the dig should misguide the rod, when he again consulted it to make certain that they were indeed digging in the right place. With a small pile of metal—mostly coins, of course—set aside on a rock, they were again ready to set to work.

Again the rod was consulted and this time Winchell "impressed on them the occasion was one of 'awful moment,' that there was a 'divinity' guarding the treasure, and that if there was any lack of faith in any one of the party, or any should utter a word while removing the stone and taking out the chest, this divinity would put the money forever beyond their reach, and besides he could not be answerable for the consequences."

Far into the night, the silent men pried and lifted away at a stone so large they would, in their saner moments, have considered it impossible to move. Finally and inevitably, the spell was broken. "Some one of the party stepped on the foot of another, the latter crying out in pain, 'Get off from my toes!' Winchell then exclaimed in a loud voice, 'The money is gone, flee for your lives!' Every man of the party dropped his bar or lever and ran as though it was for life."

Winchell, in the dim light of his candle lantern, stood among the piles of dirt and scattered bars and shovels, smiling faintly as he watched his companions disappear. He picked up the small pile of coins and dropped them into his pocket. Middletown, he was assuring himself, might be good for a lot of fun. Then he picked up his lantern and headed back for Ezekiel Perry's house.

"Soon after this affair," the historian wrote, "Winchell made the acquaintance of the Woods who . . . were then ripe for just such a scheme . . . They swallowed Winchell, rod and all."

Leader of the Wood family was "Priest" Nathaniel Wood, embittered through rejection by the local Congregational church, to whose pulpit he had hoped to receive a call. Certain of his own divine inspiration and the absolute rightness of his private religious beliefs, he was hardly a man whom local Congregationalists could have found congenial. "He regarded himself and his followers as modern Israelites or Jews, under the special care of Providence; that the Almighty would not only specially interpose in their behalf, but would visit their enemies, the Gentiles (all outsiders) with his wrath and vengeance."

Made-to-order victims for a con man, the Woods, father and sons, were soon using the rod both to locate sites of treasures and to find answers to all sorts of queries. Winchell, keeping in the background lest the excitement come to the attention of people beyond the confines of Middletown, was a moving spirit in all this. Later it was suggested that this gave him a chance to get into circulation a number of his counterfeited coins which the Woods were ready to swear came direct from the Almighty.

> Jacob Wood, known as Capt. Wood, one of the sons of Nathaniel, was the leader in the use of the rod. "Priest Wood," his father, seemed to throw his whole soul into the rod delusion, but his use of the rod was mostly as a me-

dium of revelation. It was "St. John's rod" he said and undoubtedly was very convenient for him, as he was much
more fruitful in his prophecies than before—but Capt.
Jacob was the man to find where the money was buried,
and to use the rod at their public meetings . . . and
whenever they desired any information. If any one was
sick, they sought the rod to know whether they would live
or die, and to know what medicine to administer to them.
. . .

The greatest part of their digging for money was on . . .
the farm on which I was born and raised. There are seven
or eight places which still [1862] bear the marks of their
diggings. At one place in the "notch," it has been said they
dug to the depth of seventy feet, and from the appearances
about the place, I should judge they might have gone to
that depth . . . Many of the old people have told me that
almost every day during the season, Capt. Wood could be
seen, with the two prongs twisted around his hands, in
search for buried treasures.

Whether they were digging for and expected to find coin
or ore, has often been asked of me. They talked most about
money, which they said had been buried in this region,
which would mean coin, of course, but my opinion is that
they had become so deluded that they had no distinct idea
whether they were in pursuit of gold and silver in coin or
in its natural state . . . there was no show of reason in the
affair from beginning to end, their idea was that it was
revelation, that it was made known to them through the
medium of St. John's rod, and would be revealed to none
others than God's chosen people.

Winchell, the town historian believed, was actively behind all this,
though how he stage-managed it is not suggested. Possibly it got
out of his control, though it could always afford him a good laugh in
an otherwise-too-dull little town. Certainly, whether he was per-
sonally involved in all the bizarre episodes or not, they continued to
follow a pattern set by him—as in the Barber farm episode.

"They dug some time in a cellar on the Barber farm; there they
came to a stone and under it a chest of money, as they said. They
run their bars down, and they would strike the chest; then they
would dig awhile—run their bars down again, and it would not be
there. This would be repeated—sometimes the chest would be
there, and then it would not. Once they raised it up and were on the
point of taking it out when their efforts became powerless. The chest
would come no further." The 'chest," one guesses, was a dirt-

covered squarish stone such as could be encountered in that heavily slate-producing region.

Never doubting the authenticity of the chest, "they then laid a Bible upon it, and went after someone to come and pray over it, but when they returned the Bible and the chest of money were both gone. This result they said was owing to the wickedness or want of faith in some one or more of the party." Suspicion, apparently, never focused upon Winchell.

Actually, it needed no Winchell to keep the dowsing, once started, moving in weird directions, such as recounted in an incident involving two young ladies of Middletown "who had hitherto sustained a good moral character. They had it revealed to them by the rods (as they thought) that the devil was in their clothing, and by the direction of the rod, their clothing was taken off, and they, in a winter night, went across the mountain into Poultney." Nothing is said as to whether the young ladies were permitted shawls from which the devil might have been properly exorcised. In any case, after their eight-mile walk, they did encounter devil-free clothing—and lived to tell the tale.

Perhaps the devil was finding the Middletown-Poultney line a very interesting place wherein to linger. Presently "a young lady by the name of Ann Bishop mysteriously disappeared; no one could find any clue as to her whereabouts." Clearly this was a matter in which to consult the Woods and their rods. The captain promptly brought his rod and "it pointed to a certain place in Wells Pond, which runs up into the south part of Poultney. The conclusion was that the lady was drowned in that place, and the next thing done was a preparation to get the body. Ropes, chains and hooks were procured, and logs were drawn up, a horse blanket and some other matter, but no human body. She had drowned there, the rods-men said, they were sure of that." There is no record as to how they explained away that certainty when, some time after, Ann Bishop turned up alive and well.

At another time, the Woods "had it revealed to them that they must build a temple. They got out the timber for the frame, got it raised up to the rafters, when they had another revelation that the work must be discontinued, and nothing more was done on the temple." A convenient way for ending work that was becoming too laborious!

By the time December, 1800, came round,

> it became evident that a crisis would soon be reached. Priest Wood was becoming so loud and vehement and so frenzied in his favorite theme of God's judgement upon wicked Gentiles, that it was not difficult to perceive that a paroxysm and collapse were near at hand. It was revealed to them, as they said, that on a certain night there would

be an earthquake—that immediately prior to the earthquake, the "destroyer" would pass through the land and slay a portion of the unbelievers, and the earthquake would complete the destruction of them and their worldly possessions. The day on which they predicted that this would occur was the 14th day of January, A.D. 1801.

When the day arrived for the earthquake, the Woods and their friends all collected at the house of Nathaniel Wood, Jr. . . . and, as they left their own houses, prepared for the earthquake by putting their crockery on the floor, and wrote on each of their doorposts: "Jesus, our passover was sacrificed for us." . . . One of their duties on the occasion was to determine who were and who were not to be saved from the approaching destruction or plague, as they called it, and to admit such into the house, and those only, who were to be spared.

Suddenly there was borne in upon the more level-headed townspeople the danger of an obsession they had previously watched with indulgent amusement. Suppose some of those self-styled Israelites should fancy themselves called upon to act as destroying angels, put selected Gentiles to the sword, and maybe even get up an artificial earthquake, using gunpowder whose storage place—under the pulpit of the Congregational Church—might present a special challenge to Nathaniel Woods, Sr. In the light of recent wild happenings, this was not beyond the realm of possibility. It was well to be prepared.

Capt. Miner (of the Militia) stationed his company as sentinels and patrols in different parts of the town, with directions to allow no person to pass them unless a satisfactory account of themselves could be given and especially to have an eye out for "destroying angels" . . . there was no sleep that night among the inhabitants; fear, consternation, great excitement and martial law prevailed throughout the night, but the morning came without any earthquake.

The only real damage to life or property that developed from that long, chill night of vigil was the destruction of Captain Jacob Wood's crockery where he had laid it on the floor. A young citizen, clearly disappointed in the tameness of an occasion that had promised so much excitement, announced, "The earthquake hadn't orter go fer nothin'!" then entered the house and used his feet to good advantage.

Other damage there was, however, and of a more enduring as

well as a profounder kind. This was to the local reputation of the Woods, whose earthquake delusion had proved to be sadly and conspicuously false. They and their followers were all now objects of ridicule—something fanatics can bear less resignedly than outright persecution.

Soon Priest Woods and his still-believing followers disappeared from the environs of Middletown to carry on their deluded ways, folk said, somewhere in western New York State. Winchell had already begun to find that his little game had gotten out of hand and was drawing uncomfortable outside attention upon his refuge, if that was truly what Middletown was for him. Certainly, he suddenly disappeared, taking his talents to some place where they might again be given full scope.

For long, though, Middletown was not the place which once it had been. Wherever two or more citizens came together, conversation was bound to turn upon the stranger and the happenings in which he had played so interesting a part. Why had he come to their quiet respectable little town? Who was he, really? That counterfeiter Wingate who was wanted in Bradford? Had he presumed to consider their Middletown a good place to practice his questionable art? If so, where had he done his work and how?

When, sometime later, on premises once belonging to Jacob Wood, someone came upon a large oven "which bore the marks of use for other purposes than baking bread," citizens were convinced they now had an answer to their riddle. With or without the connivance of the Woods clan, Winchell had there been practicing his black counterfeiting art. How he could have contrived to dispose of the large supply of coins thus created in an area where pocket money was a rarity was something no one really tried to answer. No one, moreover, thought to suggest that Winchell could have found reward enough in the satisfaction of so thoroughly leading astray so many small-town citizens who looked upon the furriner in their midst with smug disdain.

10

Vermonters were, from the start, very conscious of the value of personal liberty. Whether it was the kind of man who undertook to subdue the wilderness with his own hands or the struggle wherein Vermont settlers became helpless middlemen between authorities in New Hampshire and New York, most of them felt very strongly that all human beings must be free to plan their own lives.

As early as 1777 Captain Ebenezer Allen, a cousin of the generally more famous Allens, was faced with a decision in a matter which was to climax nearly a century later. A young Negro woman with her child had been taken prisoner from British troops somewhere near Lake Champlain and brought to Captain Allen's headquarters in Pawlet. Captain Allen promptly issued the now-famous document:

> 28 November, 1777—Headquarters Pollet,
> To whom it may concern: Know ye Whereas Dinah Mattis, a negro woman with nancey her Child of two months was taken Prisoner on Lake Champlain with the British Troops Some where near Col. Gilliner's Patten the Twelfth day of Instant November by a Scout under my Command, and according to the Resolve Past by the Honorable Continental Congress that all Prisses [Prisoners] belong to the Captiva-

tors thereof—I being Conscientious that it is not Right in the Sight of God to Keep Slaves—I therefore obtain Leave of the Detachment under my Command to give the said Dinah Mattis and Nancy her child their freedom to pass and Repass any where through the United States of America with her Behaving as becometh and to Trade and Traffick for Self and Child as tho she was Born free without being Mollested by any Person or Persons.

In Witness whereunto I have Set my hand or subscribe my name.

(signed) Ebeneze'r Allen, Capt.

In 1777, the independent republic of Vermont, which did not elect to join the Union until 1791, was including in its constitution a prohibition of slavery within its limits. It would be another three years before any of the original thirteen states chose to follow Vermont's lead. Such an attitude, of course, alarmed citizens of slave-holding states, who feared to see their property trooping north. Early in 1793 representatives of southern states pushed through Congress the first Fugitive Slave Law, which, among other stipulations, empowered the owner of an escaped slave to have that slave seized, brought before a magistrate, and delivered to his or her owner. A $500 fine was to be imposed on anyone assisting such a slave to escape or hindering the owner in attempts to regain possession.

Fugitive Slaves

Independent Vermonters still persisted in lending aid to escaping slaves. About the year 1816 Judge Theophilus Harrington of Middlebury was called upon to deliver up a fugitive slave. He told the owner that "nothing less than a bill of sale from the Almighty would suffice for him to recognize ownership of slaves as valid."

Most Vermonters were proud of Judge Harrington, but there were other, less high-minded officials who delivered slaves back into bondage. Public indignation was thus aroused until in 1843 the Vermont State Legislature made it more costly to obey the federal law than to disobey it. An act was passed "for the protection of personal liberty [of the fugitive] . . . No officer was to seize, arrest, or detain or aid in seizing, arresting, or detaining any person who might be claimed as a fugitive from labor . . . Any judge, magistrate or citizen offending against these provisions should forfeit a sum of not more than $1000 and be confined in the State Prison for not more than five years." The rights of habeas corpus and trial by jury were not to be denied any human being, regardless of color.

Reverend Haynes

It certainly could have been no handicap to citizens who maintained that no human being had any right to own another's person that a highly skilled and respected mulatto preacher by the name of Lemuel Haynes had been living and preaching in Vermont. Born and raised in Connecticut, in 1775 he volunteered as a Minuteman and presently served in the expedition to Fort Ticonderoga. Largely self-taught, Haynes (1753-1833) eventually received an honorary degree from Middlebury College. His quick wit and sharp repartee gave him a special fame, and anecdotes about him became common currency.

One such anecdote runs: "He went one evening into a store where liquor was drank, as well as sold. In his pleasant manner, he addressed the company, 'How d'ye do? How do you all do here?' The merchant, willing to joke a little, replied, 'O, not more than half drunk.' 'Well, well,' said Mr. Haynes, 'I'm glad that a reformation has begun.'"

Another story tells of two young men who came to him asking, "Father Haynes, have you heard the good news?"

"No," said Haynes, "What is it?"

"It is great news indeed," said one of them, "and if it is true, your business is at an end."

"What is it?" repeated Mr Haynes.

"Why," said the first, "the devil is dead."

Lifting up his hands and placing one on the head of each young man, he repeated in a tone of deep concern, "Oh! Poor fatherless children! What will become of you!"

Antislavery Sentiment

Antislavery sentiment was kept alive by a paper called *The Voice of Freedom*, first published in 1839, six years after Rev. Haynes' death:

> Though an individual enterprise, *The Voice of Freedom* was regarded as an organ of the then recently formed Anti-Slavery Society of the State, of which Rowland T. Robinson, of Ferrisburg, was president . . . As yet the anti-slavery sentiment of the State had not taken the form of political action, and only sought to promote its objects by moral and religious methods. But recent events had given a new impetus to the movement.

Both the president of that society and the editor of its presumed organ, one Joseph Poland, were already actively engaged in that unique transportation network commonly known as "the underground railroad." Since it was strictly illegal to assist runaway slaves, any records kept of its functioning were soon destroyed. In 1898 a book appeared in which the author had collected what facts he could and corresponded with many people all over the northern states whose families had been involved in this risky and dangerous undertaking.

The Underground Railroad

Some of these underground railroad lines ran through Vermont:

> Rev. Joshua Young was receiving agent at Burlington, Vermont, and testifies that during his residence there, he and his friend and parishioner, L. H. Bigelow, did "considerable business." South of Burlington, there was a series of stations . . . The names of these stations have been obtained from Mr. Rowland E. Robinson, whose father's house was a refuge for fugitives at Ferrisburg, Vermont, and from the Hon. Joseph Poland, the editor of the first anti-slavery newspaper in the State, who himself was an agent of the Underground Road in Montpelier. The names are those of nine towns, which form a line roughly parallel to the west boundary of the state, namely, North Ferrisburg, Ferrisburg, Vergennes, Middlebury, Brandon, Rutland, Wallingford, Manchester and Bennington . . . Bennington being at the southern extremity where escaped slaves were received from Troy, New York. The terminal at the northern end of this route was St. Albans, whence runaways could be hastened across the Canadian frontier.

The eastern Vermont branch started at Brattleboro and ran through Chester, Woodstock, Randolph, "and intermediate points" to Montpelier, where the line divided, going either through Burlington or Newport or Morristown. Hundreds of fugitives passed through and relatively few were retaken because of the astonishingly effective organization of the dedicated folk who passed runaways on from one station to another.

Inevitably this roused indignation among those who were thus losing both property and labor. In 1850 the United States Congress passed a Fugitive Slave Law stronger in its provisions and penalties than that of 1793. Far from intimidating Vermonters, this so aroused them that any agent who publicly took human property into custody was likely to face a mob of aroused citizens.

In 1892, Rowland E. Robinson (mentioned above) published his

Vermont, *A Study of Independence*, in which he reflects the atmosphere of his childhood home:

> The star-guided fugitive might well feel an assurance of liberty when his foot touched the soil that in old days had given freedom to Dinah Mattis and her child, and draw a freer breath in the state whose judge in later years demanded of a master, before his runaway slave would be given up to him, that he should produce a bill of sale from the Almighty.

Today, the comfortable slave room of Rowland Robinson's home in Ferrisburg can still be visited. This was just one of many stations on the underground line, which, Robinson wrote, "held its hidden way through Vermont, along which many a dark skinned passenger secretly travelled, concealed during the day in quiet stations, at night passing from one to another, helped onward by friendly hands until he reached Canada and gained the protection of that government which in later years was to become the passive champion of his rebellious master."

Throughout all the Canadian border states underground railroads were functioning, the list of known agents being long. Of all those states, however, Vermont was to be the only one destined to become a battlefield, if only briefly, of the forthcoming war which Vermonters persisted in calling "The Rebellion."

The St. Albans Raid

The raid of October 19, 1864, having given to the town a notoriety, greater than any event which ever occurred within its bounds before or since, an accurate and full account will be expected in this place. A band of armed and desperate ruffians, in the interest of the slaveholders' rebellion, 22 in number, succeeded, by a secret and well planned movement, in robbing our banks in open daylight, and in escaping to their base of operations in Canada with their plunder . . .

Our people, like those of New England villages generally, were occupied upon the day in question with their private affairs . . . with no suspicion of danger, and with scarcely a weapon of defence. The rebel plan was indeed a bold one, and is conceded to have been ably and skillfully carried out . . .

Bennett H. Young, who it appeared afterward was the leader [of the raiders], accompanied by two others, came to town from St. Johns in Canada, Oct. 10, and put up at the

Tremont-house. Two others, on the same day, stopped at the American Hotel, and, on the next day, were followed by three others. These men were (most of them at least) in and about the village up to the time of the raid, occupied in ascertaining the habits of the people, the situation of the banks and location of their safes—also the places where horses could be easiest obtained, when they should be ready to leave. They attracted no more attention than other strangers, who arrive more or less on every train, and put up at the hotels. One of those who stopped at the Tremont, was remarked as a diligent reader of the Scriptures, and was repeatedly heard reading aloud, an hour at a time. One of the charitable lady boarders took him to be a student of theology.

In order to ascertain to what extent fire-arms were possessed by the people, they made a fruitless endeavor to borrow guns for the alleged purpose of hunting. They called at the stores, making enquiries for trifling articles, entering into conversation freely with the proprietors and others. Young visited the residence of Gov. Smith and politely desired the privilege of looking over the grounds and inspecting the horses in the stables, which was accorded him. Oct. 18, two more came to breakfast at the Tremont, and were joined by four more at dinner. The greater part of these men were afterward identified as those who had been boarding at the hotels in St. Johns in Canada, for some days previous.

On the 19th, the day of the raid, five came to dinner at the American and six at the St. Albans House . . . Two came in a carriage from Burlington and the others alighted from the Montreal train, which arrived at noon. They differed in nothing from ordinary travellers except that they had side valises or satchels, depending from a strap over the right shoulder. They had learned that Tuesday, being market day, would be an unfavorable one for their purpose, but that the day following would be the dullest of the week, when there would probably be but very few people in the streets. It so happened that this particular Wednesday, nearly 40 of the active men of the town were in Montpelier, in attendance upon the legislature, then in session, and at Burlington, awaiting the progress of important cases before the supreme court. . . .

The raiders . . . were mostly young men of from 20 to 26 years. The afternoon of Wednesday, Oct. 19th, was cloudy, threatening rain, and the streets were particularly quiet . . . Immediately after the town clock had struck the hour of three, the banks were entered, simultaneously, by men with revolvers concealed upon their persons. Collins, Spurr and Teavis, with two others, entered the St. Albans Bank. C. N. Bishop, the teller, sat by a front window, counting and assorting bank notes, when the men entered, and going to the counter to see what they wanted, two of them pointed two pistols, each of large size, at his head, upon which he sprang into the director's room in the rear, in which was Martin I. Seymour, another clerk, engaged with the books.

Bishop, with Seymour, endeavored to close the door, but it was forced open with violence by the robbers, who seized them by the throat, pointing pistols at their heads, and saying in a loud whisper, "Not a word—we are confederate soldiers—have come to take your town—have a large force—we shall take your money, and if you resist, will blow your brains out—we are going to do by you, as Sheridan has been doing by us in the Shenandoah valley."

Revenge may have added to their courage but their primary object was funds for the dwindling Confederate treasury—not the last time that a bank robbery was to be justified on ideological grounds.

On being told that resistance would not be made, they relaxed their hold, but with pistols still pointed, they kept guard over their prisoners, while the others proceeded rapidly to gather up and stow away, in their pockets and valises, the bank notes on Bishop's table and in the safe. A drawer under the counter containing $9000 they failed to discover. Bags of silver containing $1500 were hauled out, from which they took about $400, saying the whole was too heavy to take. While this was going on, the handle of the outside door was turned and one of the robbers admitted . . . a merchant of the village, with $393 in his hand, who had come to pay a note. A robber presented the pistol at his breast and said, "I will take that money." . . . Just after this, a clerk of Joseph Weeks came in with $210 in a bank book to deposit. This was taken and the astonished boy dragged into the director's room with the others . . .

The robbers had found but a few hundred dollars in United States bonds, and no gold . . . With the inevitable pistol pointed at his breast, Mr. Seymour was severely interrogated as to their United States bonds and gold. They failed, however, to intimidate him into any confession that there were either gold or bonds in the bank. In the safe, through which they nervously fumbled, was a large amount of U.S. bonds in envelopes, belonging to private individuals and which had been deposited for safe keeping. The coolness of Mr. Seymour saved these parties some $50,000. The robbers also overlooked, in their great haste, a bundle of St. Albans bank notes in sheets, regularly signed, but which had not been cut apart for use, to the amount of $50,000. It seems that they actually left behind more money than they took from the bank. This happened probably from their being excited with liquor. They brought with them into the bank a rank atmosphere of alcholic fumes, adding another to the many proofs, already on record, of the intimate connection between ardent spirits and crime.

The entire time occupied in the robbery of this bank did not exceed 12 minutes. Hearing a report of firearms, three went out. Two staid a few moments and backed out, with pistols pointed at their prisoners.

Meanwhile five of the raiders were in the Franklin County Bank, four more soon following. They drew their revolvers and threatened clerk Beardsley with, "We are confederate soldiers. There are a hundred of us. We have come to rob your bank and burn your town . . . We want all your greenbacks, bills and property of every description."

They came behind the counter and into the vault, taking possession of everything they supposed valuable. When they had secured their booty and were ready to leave, [raider] Hutchinson told Mr. Beardsley that he must go into the vault, where Clark [a customer] had already been placed. Mr. Beardsley remonstrated against an act so inhuman, told him that the vault was air-tight, and that no man could live long in it, that he had got all their money and that if left out, he would make no alarm. This did not move the savage in the least. He seized his unresisting prisoner by the arm, led him into the vault, and fastened the door. Beardsley supposed they would carry into execution their threat to burn the town, and had before his imagination the horrid prospect of being burned alive. Hearing voices in the room, he rattled the iron door of his prison and soon heard his name called . . . He told how the door could be opened and was then released, his confinement having lasted 20 minutes. As he emerged from the bank, he saw the robbers galloping off in a body to the north.

Similar events were taking place at the same time in the First National Bank. An uncomprehending witness there was General John

Nason, "an old man, then nearly 90 years of age, and very deaf," who "sat during the entire transaction in the back part of the room reading a newspaper. After the robbers had gone out, he came forward and mildly enquired, 'What gentlemen were those?' "

Thirteen of the robbers had been engaged in rifling the banks. The others had been occupied in guarding the streets. The banks were all situated on Main Street, in a space not exceeding 45 rods. It was important not to allow any information to be carried out of this locality. At a short distance down Lake Street were the machine shops and depot buildings of the railroad where hundreds of men were at work, who if made aware of what was doing, would have quickly disposed of the entire rebel party. They therefore stopped all persons who essayed to pass out of Main Street by threats of instant death, and ordered them to pass to the green in front of the American [hotel] . . .

Some of the robbers now commenced the seizure of horses with which to effect an escape. Field's livery stable was first visited. Opposition to the appropriation of horses being made by Mr. Field, a shot was instantly fired on him by Mr. Young, the ball passing through his hat. Mr. Shepard of Highgate, driving a pair of horses in a double

wagon, was stopped opposite the Franklin County Bank and his horses taken. The harness was quickly stripped off and the robbers mounted without saddles, using the head-stalls for bridles . . . Young rode up and down the street, directing the operations of his fellow-robbers, ordering people into their houses, or to take a stand on the green. A man started off when Young called out, "What is that man running for? Where the hell is he going to? Shoot the damned cuss!" and several shots were fired. . . .

Young frequently ordered his men to throw Greek fire upon the wooden buildings. This was a phosphoric com-pound in a liquid state. A bottle of it was thrown against the front of N. Atwood's store, but without much effect. The water closet of the American was besmeared with the same compound. It burned until the next day; but as the wood-work was kept wet, it did no damage.

The robbers now began to move towards the north, and halted near the corner of Main and Bank streets. Bedard's shop was rifled of saddles, bridles and blankets. Seven horses were led out of Fuller's livery stable . . . In front of Jaquez grocery store, a horse was hitched . . . a robber had mounted the horse . . . The alarm was now becom-ing general, the robbers were mounted and were shooting in every direction . . . The robbers, finding the street rapidly filling, formed in sections of four and galloped off to the north . . .

The raiders took the road to Sheldon, making all the speed possible. At the village, they dashed across the bridge over the creek and then attempted to set it on fire. They had intended to rob the bank at this place, but found it closed; and as they were apprehensive of pursuit, they contented themselves with stealing a horse from Col. Keith and passed on to Canada, crossing the Missisquoi at Enosburgh Falls. A party of our citizens started in pursuit as soon as horses and arms could be procured; but one half an hour went by before they were ready to move.

A laughable incident occurred on the way to Sheldon. Just this side of the village, in the woods, they met a farmer on a good substantial horse which one of them wanted in exchange for the one he was riding, which was near giving out. Without words or ceremony, they drew the aston-ished farmer from his horse, which one of them quickly mounted, leaving his own jaded, panting animal in its place, when they dashed off rapidly as before. In mute and puzzled amazement, the farmer remained standing in the road, until the St. Albans party, riding like the others at full speed, came in sight. He, supposing them to be another portion of the body by whom he had been robbed, ran for life across the field, and the St. Albans party, recognizing the horse and mistaking him for one of the robbers, gave chase, firing repeatedly at him, and gave it up only when their further progress was checked by swampy ground.

The robbers succeeded in getting across the line into Canada, but thirteen were arrested there and held for trial. The money found upon them amounted to some $80,000. The prisoners were brought before Justice Coursol, and after a long and tedious examination, at great expense to the banks and the U.S. government, he, on the 13th of December arrived at the conclusion that he possessed no jurisdiction in the matter, ordered the men to be discharged and the stolen money restored to them. Applause was manifested in the courtroom at this decision, but the infamous judge had a sense of decency remaining sufficient to order it be suppressed.

The murderous ruffians left the court room in triumph, and were received in the streets by their sympathizing Canadian friends with cheers. Lamothe, the Montreal chief of police, anticipating, or having been notified in advance of the judge's decision, had the money of which he was custodian ready to deliver, and having received it, the party left immediately. . . .

The Canadian government, it is believed, did not sympathize with these magistrates in their decisions. The governor-general, Lord Monck, recommended to the Provincial Parliament to appropriate $50,000 in gold, to be paid to the banks as an equivalent for the money found upon the captured robbers, and which had been restored to them by the order of Judge Coursol. This was voted by the parliament and paid to the banks, and was the equivalent to $88,000 in currency. The entire amount taken by the robbers was $208,000. The loss was therefore $120,000. To this might be added a sum not less than $20,000 which was expended in the arrest of the robbers, and in attempting to secure their extradition.

St. Albans survived the loss. Companies of home guards—infantry and cavalry—moved into town and orders went out to shoot down future marauders either while in the act of robbing, or while escaping, "or, if necessary, with a view to their capture, to cross the boundary line between the United States and Canada. This order, though somewhat modified soon after by President Lincoln, was productive of good. The rebel sympathizers in Canada grew much more respectful, and manifested less disposition to encourage attacks from their side of the line upon the territory of the United States."

More likely, there were no more such raids being planned, for that $120,000 was bound to prove but a drop in the bucket for the Confederate treasury. The war was already winding to a close. For both sides, it was not the money but the human loss that was to become most evident.

In Vermont, as elsewhere, the finest youth had thrown themselves into the war which had so roused their state's sympathies. Eighteen-year-old John Tyler, for instance, wrote his father (Justice Royall Tyler's son) in 1861, asking permission to enlist. His father promptly replied, "My dear John:—If you do not enlist, you will be ashamed hereafter to look your children in the face . . ." There would be no children to look in the face; John died from wounds in May, 1864. Of all the men who went forth to war, nearly half never returned to live in Vermont. Half of that half had died from wounds or disease; the remainder, having learned of the West, followed their ancestors' examples and took up residence in new lands.

No one will question that while settlers were moving into Vermont, men and women were meeting, mating, and raising families. Though by now many of their descendants may have disappeared into other states, the testimony of rows of slim and slanting headstones in old cemeteries is incontrovertible. That people were falling in love according to timeless patterns but courting according to their own might be concluded by readers who have progressed this far in the book.

If they could talk, the headstones of the Kelsey burial plot in Salisbury might recount an interesting tale. The town historian tells it simply:

> Jonathan Titus and Elizabeth Kelsey had appointed their wedding day. A brother of Elizabeth died. They indefinitely postponed the event; but after the service of burial, the father of the deceased and of the bride suggested the marriage should be there solemnized, whereupon Mr. Prindle, the officiating clergyman, standing at the head of the new-made grave, and the bride and groom at the foot, the astonished audience witnessed a bridal among the tombs.

An imaginative reader might see in this stark account the young couple's despairing glances and the kind father's compassion. Or they might decide the father was notably parsimonious and was trying to get double service from the clergyman for a single fee and to avoid the additional cost of a planned wedding celebration. Surely readers must agree that romance in Vermont, though as real as elsewhere, could follow entirely original patterns.

Ethan Allen's Bride

Ethan Allen, certainly, seems to have been as original in his approach to matrimony as to military affairs and religion. His first wife Mary, a somewhat shrewish ailing woman who had come with him into the grants, died of lingering consumption in early 1783. Within a year Ethan was in Westminster, on the far side of the republic of Vermont from his home in Sunderland. There he met and fell in love with the beautiful young widow, Fanny Buchanan. She had come to Westminster with her mother, Mrs. Patrick Wall, to claim lands left to mother and daughter by the will of Fanny's Yorker stepfather— Fanny to receive one third. In the *History of Eastern Vermont* Mr. Benjamin Hall tells at length of the encounter between the recent Green Mountain Boy and the young woman, little more than half his age, who was claiming lands willed her by a notorious Yorker.

> She was a dashing woman, and early attracted the attention of the quiet townspeople to whom a bearing as imperious as that which she exhibited was wholly new. During some one of his frequent visits to Westminster, Gen. Ethan Allen, at that time a widower, formed an acquaintance which subsequently ripened into a warm, but, for a time, singularly intermittent friendship. Pleased with the originality of his views and conversation; flattered at her own ability to arrest the attention of a man whom all feared, but whom few loved; and imagining that she should find more sympathy in the companionship of his strong, active nature, than in the society of those by whom she was surrounded, Mrs. Buchanan found herself on some occasions irresistibly attracted towards him.
>
> John Norton, the tavern keeper at Westminster, and a man of considerable note, said to her one day, "Fanny, if you marry General Allen, you will be the queen of a new State!"
>
> "Yes," she replied ". . . if I should marry the devil, I would be queen of hell!"
>
> . . . By one who knew her well, she is said to have been a fascinating woman; endowed with an ease of manner

which she had acquired in the polite society of that day
. . . possessed of a refined taste and many accomplishments, and on most occasions, soft and gentle in her ways
and speech. The aversion with which she occasionally
regarded General Allen, disappeared, at length, in the
stronger admiration which she entertained for him, and
she consented to become his wife. The circumstances attendant upon their marriage, which occurred previous to
the year 1784, were novel, and fully characteristic of the
man who cared but little either for "forms of government"
or for the social customs of life.

Soon after the removal of General Stephen R. Bradley to
Westminster, he erected a convenient dwelling for himself
and family on the flat, north of the spot where the old
Court-house formerly stood. During the sessions of the
Surpreme court, the judges usually boarded with him. At
this period, Mrs. Wall and her daughter Mrs. Buchanan,
occupied rooms in the house, and General Allen was a
frequent visitor. One morning, while General Bradley and
the judges were at breakfast, General Allen, with his
sleigh, horses, and driver, appeared at the gate, and, on
coming into the room, was invited to partake. He
answered, that he had breakfasted at Norton's, and would,
while they were engaged, step into Mrs. Wall's apartments
and see the ladies. Entering without ceremony, he found
Mrs. Buchanan in a morning-gown, standing on a chair,
and arranging some articles on the upper shelves of a china
closet. After recognizing her informal visitor, Mrs.
Buchanan raised up a cracked decanter, and calling
General Allen's attention to it, accompanied the exhibition
with a playful remark. The General laughed at the sally,
and after some little chat, said to her, "If we are to be married, now is the time, for I am on my way to Arlington."
"Very well," she replied, descending from the chair, "but
give me time to put on my Joseph."

Meanwhile, the judges and their host, having finished
their breakfast, were smoking their long pipes. While thus
engaged the couple came in, and General Allen, walking
up to his old friend Chief Justice Moses Robinson, addressed him as follows:—"Judge Robinson, this young
woman and myself have concluded to marry each other,
and to have you perform the ceremony." "When?" said
the Judge, somewhat surprised. "Now!" replied Allen.
"For myself," he continued, "I have no great opinion of
such formality, and from what I can discover, she thinks as
little of it as I do. But as a decent respect for the opinions of

mankind seems to require it, you will proceed." "General," said the Judge, "this is an important matter, and have you given it a serious consideration?" "Certainly," replied Allen, "but," glancing at Mrs. Buchanan, "I do not think it requires much consideration." The ceremony then proceeded, until the Judge inquired of Ethan whether he promised to live with Frances "agreeable to the law of God." "Stop! stop!" cried Allen at this point. Then pausing, and looking out of the window, the pantheist exclaimed, "The law of God as written in the great book of Nature? Yes! Go on!" The Judge continued, and when he had finished, the trunk and guitarcase of Mrs. Allen were placed in the sleigh, the parties took their leave and were at once driven off to the General's home. Thus did the stepdaughter of Crean Brush become the wife of the man for whose apprehension Governor Tryon, at the instigation of Brush, had on the 9th of March, 1774, offered a reward of £100.

The Nude Bride

Westminster, at that date, seems to have become a place for originality in romance. Widow Lovejoy, whose husband had died without paying his debts, was appointed administratrix of the practically nonexistent estate. Wrote one historian:

> At this early period certain people were led to believe that whoever should marry a widow, who was administratrix upon the estate of her deceased husband, and should through her come in possession of anything that had been purchased by the deceased husband, would become adminstrator in his own wrong, and render himself liable to answer for the goods and estate of his predecessor. The method adopted to avoid this difficulty, in the marriage of Asa Averill of Westminster to his second wife, the widow of Major Peter Lovejoy, was very singular. By the side of the chimney in the widow's house was a recess of considerable size. Across this a blanket was stretched in such a manner as to form a small inclosure. Into this Mrs. Lovejoy passed with her attendants, who completely disrobed her, and threw her clothes into the room. She then thrust her hand through a small aperture purposely made in the blanket. The proffered member was clasped by Mr. Averill, and in this position he was married to the nude widow on the other side of the woollen curtain. He then produced a complete assortment of wedding

attire which was slipped into the recess. The new Mrs. Averill soon after appeared in full dress, ready to receive the congratulations of the company, and join in their hearty rustic festivities. The marriage proved a happy one, their children by their former partners living in great harmony, not only with each other but with those also who were afterwards born to the new pair.

The Way of a Bachelor

A man who arrived in the grants as a bachelor had his own kind of problem, especially if his pitch was isolated. In the 1780s Dr. Jonathan Arnold of St. Johnsbury became acutely aware of this. Once, after journeying down the river to Barnet, where he passed the night with Enos Stevens, also a bachelor, the two got to talking about the forlorn situation of

> pioneers in a new settlement . . . hopelessly destitute of wives . . . an expedition to Charleston (N.H.) was immediately planned to take effect on the morrow, the object being to spy out the available daughters of the land.
>
> Arrived in Charleston, they called on Samuel Stevens, Esq., and made known their wishes. After some consultation, invitations were issued to Cynthia Hastings and Sophy Grout requesting their company at tea, it being understood by the contrivers of the plot, that the two strangers from Vermont should accompany them back to their homes . . . It was judged advisable that Mrs. Squire West should also be in attendance to play the part of umpire in case both gentlemen should claim the same lady.
>
> Tea time arrived and so did the unsuspecting maidens. The evening passed, but when the hour of departure came, Cynthia Hastings seemed to be in double demand. The ladies still remained in blissful ignorance of the conspiracy. Mrs. Squire West . . . very sagely argued that Sophy Grout was admirably adapted to be the companion of a farmer (Mr. Stevens was a tiller of the soil) but as for Cynthia, it was much more suitable that she should be attended by a professional man. This wise deci..on of Mrs. Squire West (especially grateful to Dr. Arnold) prevailed, and before separating that night each of the gentlemen . . . made known the special object of their visit.

The girls were persuaded. Sophy's father, however, raised objections when he learned Stevens was a Tory. He told his daughter that if she persisted in her intentions of marrying Enos Stevens, she should have nothing but a cow for a dowry. A few days later, the "afflicted Grout family" had to witness the departure of daughter Sophy with her Tory and the cow.

The Ways of Parents

Dr. Arnold might have been spared his journey in search of a mate had he had a father or known a father like the man who became a settler in remote Charleston (Vermont), only a few miles south of the Canadian border.

> The story has been handed down to grand- and great-grandchildren that grandfather Page . . . had the forethought to hire 12 active, smart young men to penetrate the forests with himself and family, to fell the trees and do the work of making a new settlement. Whether the old gentleman took this job into his own hands in the old Patriarchal style of adding sons to his family, or whether the daughters were privy to the selection, tradition does not tell, but it expressly says that the 12 daughters married the 12 young men and settled all around him.

It may be that Mrs. Richardson of Mendon had something of the same sort in mind when she hired Lydia Fales:

> When Rufus Richardson was living at home, at his father's, who kept a sort of Public House in Mendon . . . his mother had to keep a hired girl, and she was a good one; her name was Lydia Fales. Rufus and Lydia took a liking to each other and agreed to get married. Both of them were great workers and very economical. They hardly could spare time to go to Rutland to get married and there was no one . . . nearer than Rutland to perform the ceremony . . . It so happened one day that Esq. Williams of Rutland, who had business to attend to in Woodstock, called at the Richardsons to go get a baiting for his horse and dinner for himself. Lydia was washing that day, and had got all done except to finish mopping the floor. She was right in the middle of that exercise, when in came Rufus and told her there was a Justice of the Peace in the other room, and proposed they should be married then, which she agreed to provided she might stand up and have the ceremony performed just as she was, without the trouble of changing her dress . . . The Justice was called in. She threw down her mop and was married. She then took up her mop and finished her work.

On the other hand, a girl thus sought might take her desirability too much for granted. When the girl Abel Rich proposed to asked to be allowed time to consider so serious a proposition, Abel generously replied, "Take all eternitee!" and departed, never to return.

The twenty-four-year-old lawyer, Luke Knowlton of Windham County, was more persistent and more successful than Abel Rich:

> In 1799 he married Charlotte, daughter of Deacon Moses . . . who was under 16 years of age. Her father opposed the match on three grounds, viz: "First, She is too young. Second—I cannot spare her. Third—I can give her no dower." To this, the young advocate replied: "First—She will grow older every day, and as fast in my hands as yours. Second—you have a wife and other daughters and can better do without her than I can. Third—It is your daughter I want and not a dower." The young lawyer won his suit.

In Randolph, Joseph Waterman, a suitor for the hand of the daughter of Deacon Flint (1746–1827)—he who had refused to encourage the installation of lightning rods on the new meeting house—was spared the necessity of pleading. Years later, Waterman recalled the deacon as

> "a very plain, blunt man." Says he, "I shall never forget asking him for your Aunt Lucy." "Why?" said I. He then said, "After school closed in Johnson, I went to Randolph to visit her. In the morning, before leaving for home, I wished to get his consent to marry her. I was not much acquainted with him, and it being a delicate subject, I watched my opportunity to see him out of doors and alone. He was in the orchard, so I went up to him and asked him if he was willing I should have his daughter Lucy. 'Oh, yes,' said he, 'you may have her and welcome, if you want her; she isn't good for anything!' and he spoke so loud that they all heard every word he said."

The delicate subject being settled in a not-so-delicate way, Joseph and Lucy were duly married.

Women's Lib—Eighteenth-Century Style

How couples got along together after marriage is generally left to the imagination. Here again, those little cemeteries tell a tale of frequent childbirth, infantile death, and also the death of mothers for whom childbirth was a hazard. If the women survived childbirth they might die of consumption, which was tragically common among early Vermont settlers. Accident, of course, was also a threat to both sexes. All these hazards survived, the pioneers might live to exceedingly ripe old age. Widows and widowers, accepting such dangers as routine, did not hesitate to remarry promptly if they could find suitable mates and sometimes, one suspects, if the available mates were not so suitable.

Quaker Wing Rogers of Danby had at least four wives in succession—Deliverance Chatman, Mercy Hatch, Rebecca Sherman, and Hannah Titus. Wing arrived in Danby in 1770 as a very early settler. He has been described as "a bold and resolute man" of large means and of notable eccentricities. One of his eccentricities displayed itself in a determined bullying of his wives. The first three seem to have taken it meekly. The fourth made up for it all in a notable manner. As the story runs:

> One day he came in from the field and ordered his wife to bring him a pitcher of water from the spring. She went cheerfully and readily and brought the water. He received it from her hand, and looking into the vessel, declined to drink, on the plea that there was a straw in it, and pouring it out ordered her to bring another. She did so and this time took extra care to ascertain that it was perfectly pure and irreproachable. Without drinking, he poured it out and ordered her to go a third time. She did so and returned: and when at a convenient distance, she dashed the whole contents over him. He spluttered and gasped at the suddenness of the cold bath; and when sufficiently recovered, he looked up at the calm, quiet countenance beside him and spoke out, "There, that's done like a sensible woman! If Becky had done that years ago, she would have made a good husband of me."

Another anecdote tells of the time "Rogers went out, turned the cows into the meadow and returning, addressed his wife, 'My dear, the cows are all in the meadow; I want thee should go and drive them out.' She started at once, like a dutiful wife, and opening the bars between the meadow and cornfield, hurried the cows through and then returned, saying, 'My dear, the cows are in the cornfield. I want thee should drive them out.'" Seeing the cows happily consuming his growing corn "was too much for Wing's acquisitiveness and he drove them back to the pasture at once."

All About Algiers

However much habits have changed through those many decades since Hannah Rogers gave Wing a foretaste of women's

lib, the ways of romance have changed very little—as witness some considerably-more-recent episodes in one of those towns nicknamed Algiers. This was at a time when a notable bestseller was *The Algerine Captive,* authored by Justice Royall Tyler. Since to readers of those times, Algiers suggested wildness, toughness, and unconventionality, a town might receive that nickname if it seemed to have those qualifications.

Bernie's Blunder

Matrimonially speaking, the year 1893 seems to have been an especially interesting one in this particular Algiers, especially to young Bernie Weed, who, right in the midst of his wedding, was arrested for cattle stealing. The assembled guests were, to put it mildly, shocked. Young Bernie had always been sober and reliable; else how would Bernie's father have left his large, prosperous farm in Bernie's care when taking off for the World's Columbian Exposition in Chicago. Without a concern for the home farm, Farmer Weed and his wife enjoyed themselves and, having delayed beyond the time originally anticipated, returned home filled with the exciting things they'd seen as was Bernie of plans for his forthcoming wedding.

Being a practical man, Farmer Weed soon went out to view the young cattle in their hillside pasture, found them thriving but—alas!—the count short by one. Someone had been taking advantage of his absence! He hastened to the constable and demanded that the thief be located, the heifer returned or paid for.

Time passed and neither heifer nor thief seemed locatable. Farmer Weed fumed. Meanwhile Bernie's wedding day arrived and, according to accepted local usage, was taking place in the bride's home before a large number of assembled guests, among whom was the constable, smiling happily. When the moment came to "speak or forever hold your peace," the constable stepped forward, laid a hand on Bernie's shoulder and arrested him for cattle stealing.

The bride fainted. Bernie's father demanded furiously who was responsible for this outrage, who dared accuse his son of such a crime. "You did," said the constable with a grin.

While murmurs of astonishment ran through the company, a justice of the peace—also a wedding guest—stepped forward, convened a justice court, and offered to hear the charges and the defense at once. Bernie remembered that his father's extended absence had left him so pinched for funds that he'd sold a young heifer to meet the most urgent bills. Being rather preoccupied with his own plans he'd neglected to mention the sale to his father, who now, flushed with embarrassment, withdrew his demands that the thief be fined and jailed.

Finally recovered from her shock and faint, the bride consented to have the wedding proceed. The couple lived happily ever after, even to the point of eventually forgiving the constable his grim practical joke.

The Reluctant Nonbrides

Other town legends deal with too coy brides-to-be. One such bride belonged to a self-consciously aristocratic family of property that prided itself on being a cut above and having traveled more widely than most of its Algiers neighbors. The author has viewed some of the family's trophies gathered on trips abroad made by past generations, and has also met Miss Aurelia, a rather handsome, dignified spinster. It was more than a bit puzzling to hear old-timers talk of "Miss Aurelia's wedding."

It seems that many years before the author set foot in Algiers there was a personable young man whose periodic business in Algiers introduced him to Miss Aurelia, a pretty and charmingly mannered young lady. Eventually the fastidious Miss Aurelia became engaged to him. She enjoyed her engagement. It was a condition that underlined her powers of attraction while demanding practically nothing of her save entertaining her fiancé (in the drawing room, of course) on his periodic visits to town. But when it came to setting the date for their wedding, she found a thousand excuses for deferring it.

The young man grew impatient as Miss Aurelia grew coyer. Finally he demanded that she free him from an engagement that was leading exactly nowhere. Miss Aurelia was horrified, seeing herself as the laughingstock of a town that had long resented the airs her family put on. So she turned on him furiously—having tried tears in vain—and said she'd sue him for breach of promise.

Of course, she had no real idea of such a public scandal. She just couldn't believe that any young man would really reject the opportunity of marrying into her family. She continued her disbelief when he replied furiously. "Very well, I'll marry you. Set the date if you wish. But I promise you now I'll never live with you."

Now, at last, wedding plans began to move. With all the pomp and ceremony imaginable in Algiers, Aurelia took the then-unusual step of arranging a real church wedding, with a home reception to follow. She looked a lovely bride and the couple was altogether handsome if the groom did look a trifle too unsmiling. Together they got into the waiting carriage to go to her home. Arrived there, he handed her down with all possible courtesy, then jumped back into the carriage and drove off, never to be seen in Algiers again.

Miss Aurelia would have done well to have followed the example set nearly a century before by spinster Ann Goodenough of Guilford. When the deacon to whom she'd been engaged had a change of mind, she accepted his decision with an expression of mild regret. He gallantly offered to "make good the damages, if she would let him know what they were." After some grave thought, she said she thought they ought to be as much as six shillings (one dollar). The thus-freed deacon "became unenviably famous by it."

This author never encountered in Algiers any old-timer who could tell the name of the man Miss Aurelia married. Miss Aurelia probably remembered but somehow the courage was never found to ask her.

The trouble with Miss Aurelia's nameless husband, her fellow-townsman Bill Loomis might have told him, was that he allowed his fiancée too much time in which to change her mind. Bill had learned the hard way by becoming engaged to a girl in Schenectady, New

York, where his own brother-in-law was mayor. The flattered girl agreed to marry him and went so far as to set the date, but when Bill arrived on that day she regretfully informed him that her mother thought her still too young for marriage. Wait six months, the two women begged.

Six months later, it seemed, the girl was a mere six months older and her mother thought that counted for nothing. Another date was set and this time Bill arrived so sure of getting married that he sported a fine new suit for the occasion. The girl's mother still insisted she was too young.

"Well!" Bill, now furious, exclaimed. "It's time for you to make the choice—your mother or me—which will it be?"

The girl wavered a bit. Then, bravely reminding herself a girl could have only one mother whereas suitors might be had by the dozen, she made the fatal choice.

Bill returned to Algiers still furious, his fury increased by the ribald jokes of which he was made the butt. Finally he retired behind the barn where, well beyond his straitlaced father's hearing, he expressed himself feelingly on the subject of women in general and that Schenectady girl in particular.

It was made even harder for Bill as he saw his pals getting married. He could hardly refuse to be present at their weddings, even though each one underlined his own unhappy state. He even undertook to escort to one wedding the new young schoolteacher who had recently arrived in town. She was pretty and she was smart and she was level-headed. Now if only that girl in Schenectady hadn't had a mother. Maybe the schoolteacher had one but she was at a safe distance . . . As they jogged home, Bill's thoughts dwelt on this.

Suddenly Bill turned to the schoolteacher and asked her if she'd marry him. After brief consideration and to Bill's utter amazement, she confessed she might. That was enough for Bill. At once he reined in his horse, turned it around, and raced back to the village, where the parson, who was relaxing after officiating at one wedding, was roused from bed to start all over again. The knot was tied then and there, and it turned out to be a long and happy marriage.

Husbands and Hornings

In Algiers, it's rarely permitted for newlyweds to settle down quietly in marriage. There's nothing quiet about the horning that almost certainly follows, as any suffering neighbor can report. Giving the couple some days (or even weeks) of grace during which they may develop a false sense of security, villagers arrive at the house very late at night after all lights are out. Nowadays they usually come in a truck provided with an assortment of musical instruments which include not only ancient horns but empty oil drums, old saws, kitchen pans, metal washboards, and other articles for making noise.

Suddenly the stillness of the country night is shattered by the most awful din anyone can imagine, and this may well keep up for hours, especially if the groom has ever been indiscreet enough to whisper that he considers hornings barbaric. Sooner or later the horners will break his spirit, coming back night after night, if necessary, until he politely provides the company with cigars and cider, preferably the hard kind.

Of course it can also happen that the learning is in the opposite direction, as the case of Herb's horning may prove. Herb's parents considered hornings altogether crude and felt it wrong to give in to horners. Herb, painfully aware of where such an attitude might lead him, whispered to his pals that his parents were elderly and needed their sleep and if he could know ahead of time, he'd meet the musical troupe at the hay barn and take care of them. He did just that.

Herb secured a barrel of hard cider and hardened it still further with applejack, spiking the whole with more than a trace of cathartic. All his horners were given cigars and told to help themselves to as much as they wanted from the barrel. They did and told Herb in somewhat blurred tones what a great fellow he was.

Those being the days when horners arrived in horse-powered vehicles, they departed in them happily—possibly a shade too happily. Soon, however, urgent calls of nature began to catch up with them and, one after another, each horner dismounted—to find himself incapable of getting back up. The sober horses, having waited in vain to hear their masters' voices, finally gave up and ambled to their respective home barns.

In the morning very early Herb hitched his team to the hay wagon and drove along the road, gathering in the still-befuddled guests who lay by the roadside. His father never learned how Herb had handled his horning, which, of course, soon became one of the legends of Algiers.

Greek Tragedy in Algiers

An occasional matrimonial happening in Algiers had the substance of Greek tragedy. A few old-timers recalled the young couple who ran a prosperous farm which the husband had inherited from the kind childless couple who had raised him. The wife was from a western state, having met and married the young man when he visited a distant relative near the town where she lived. With several healthy, highly intelligent children, it looked like a happier-than-average marriage.

Then, one day, the couple had the misfortune to be visited by an elderly gossip whose life's calling was to know everything about everyone who had ever lived in town. Ah, yes, she couldn't forget that terrible epidemic that had taken her host's parents off. So sad for the orphaned children! Oh, hadn't he been told about his sister, a so pretty child adopted by—give her a moment and she'd recall the name—they'd moved away many years ago. Ah, she had it now!

To her hosts' horror, it was the name the girl had grown up under and the couple were brother and sister. What this must have meant to a deeply religious Methodist family it is painful to imagine. All that was ever hinted to the outside world that it was truly a burden to be borne was the fact that none of those personable, gifted children ever married—possibly thinking that such a brother-sister marriage might have to be expiated by future generations.

Ways of life may change, the environment, close or remote, alter almost beyond recognition, but the people to whom the ways and that environment once belonged live on in spirit in their descendants. Still individuals, the kind of men who designed plumping mills to reduce their corn to edible meal and squirt guns to control home fires, would continue through the nineteenth century and on up to our own day to invent where necessity demanded, and to be inventive in meeting life's smaller everyday problems. Though not the exclusive possession of any group of people, it is this particular attribute which is responsible for the kind of anecdote now so often repeated as typical of Vermonters. Whomever these anecdotes may be typical of, they are certainly a matter for amusement, as those recounted so far in this book will have proved. A few more examples might be added here.

Ninepence Worth of Fun

Elderly Amos Churchill of Hubbardton told a particularly delightful tale in the course of his reminiscences:

> At a place known to fame as the Kingdom, David Chamberlain, a clerk in Horton's store, the shutters of which he

was closing for the night, happened to detect a light-fingered fellow quietly secreting a nice roll of butter in his hat, and instantly hit upon a mode of punishment.

Closing the door and addressing his victim, he said, "This is a rather cold night and something to take would do us good."

Although disposed to be off, the idea of something to take was too much for the resolution or, rather, prudence of the petty thief. Without suspicion, he took the proffered seat near the stove, which the clerk stuffed with wood, after giving him a glass of stiff West India [rum], all the while plying him with humorous and amusing talk.

It so happened that the rogue was in a corner crammed with bales and boxes, from which there was but one place of egress—and there the wily Yankee sat.

"I believe I must be going," said Ladd, for that was the culprit's name. "I have got cows to fodder and some wood to split."

He was answered by being presented with two glasses of hot rum toddy, the very sight of which would have made the hair of his head stand on end, had it not been well greased and kept down by the butter . . .

The half boozy man now began to smoke as well as to melt, and was silent as if born dumb. While, as he freely perspired, the sweat seemed of a rich yellow hue as it rolled down his face, while standing bolt upright, with his knees almost touching the red hot stove.

"Damnation cold night this!" said Chamberlain, putting more wood in the stove. "Here, let me take your hat off."

"No!" exclaimed the poor fellow at last, with a spasmodic effort to get his tongue loose; and clapping both hands on his hat, "No! Damn you, let me go! Let me out! I ain't well! Let me out!" At this stage of their proceeding, a greasy cataract is said to have poured down the poor man's face, and his inveterate tormentor was satisfied.

"Well, good night if you must go," said he. "And, neighbor, as I reckon the fun I have had out of you is worth a ninepence, I shall not charge you for that pound of butter."

The Swamp Angel

From Coventry comes a tale of a different kind.

Ammi Burrington, familiarly called "the swamp angel," was nearly 7 feet in height, broad-shouldered, long-

limbed, gaunt, skinny and crooked, with dark complexion, wide mouth, large teeth and other features to match. Tradition says that the name was given him by a Yankee peddler whom he asked to give him a ride. The peddler told him that if he would ride within the box as far as the next tavern, and remain in the box for an hour after arriving there, he should have not only a ride, but his keeping over the night. Ammi readily accepted the proposition and took his place among the tin ware. Upon arriving at the tavern the peddler announced himself as the exhibitor of "a very rare animal—the swamp angel" and proceeded to exhibit Ammi for a certain price, to his own good profit and the great amusement of the spectators.

Bald by Choice

Colonel Levi Boutwell of Montpelier was uncommonly bald and without his heavy dark wig was not recognized by people to whom otherwise he was a familiar figure.

Once he was in the washroom of the Pavilion [Hotel], and for convenience in his ablutions, had laid his wig aside. Presently a young, spruce feeling chap, with extremely red hair, came in too. Noticing the Colonel's nude head, he inquired, "Well, Uncle, why don't you have some hair on your head?" It was an impudent question . . .

Looking savagely at the red head of the saucy young stranger, the Colonel replied, "When they made me and had me all finished except my hair, they told me they had nothing left except red hair. I told them then—I Gad, I wouldn't have any. I had rather go without. They might save that for impudent young popinjays and fools."

Farmer John Brown

On December 1, 1859, when the nation's mind was on the John Brown at Harper's Ferry, Danby farmer John Brown—the grandfather of this writer's husband—was approached by a neighbor boy who begged to be given the farmer's pocketknife, "since you won't be needin' it no more."

"Why won't I be needing it?" the surprised farmer asked.

"'Cause," said the boy, for whom Harper's Ferry was neither more nor less remote than the town over the next range of hills, "'cause they're goin' to hang you tomorrow."

Grandfather Brown, whose bearded face framed in long hair gives his old photograph a strangely modern aspect, was the grandson of a first settler, from whom he inherited the original farm and the qualities that made that farming venture successful. One of those qualities was the ability to drive a good bargain without compromising his reputation for strict honesty.

A horse trader called on Grandfather Brown one day, asking whether there might be any horses for sale. When he received a negative answer he was in no way rebuffed, for he knew the ways of men like John Brown, who had a reputation for raising fine horses and for keeping the best for himself.

"What about that animal over there?" he asked, pointing across the pasture to a horse that was tossing its head in what he judged to be a spirited manner.

"You don't want that animal," the farmer told him. "She's blind in one eye and has the heaves."

The visitor, still priding himself on his judgment of horses and of men, persisted, finally offering a good price which honest farmer Brown accepted. When presently the trader discovered that farmer Brown had, indeed, been all too truthful—that the horse was blind in one eye and had the heaves—he had to admit he'd been outmaneuvered at his own trade. The joke was on him and he accepted it in good part.

One of Grandfather Brown's grandsons seemed to have inherited the family trait. He acquired a neighbor—a recently arrived twentieth-century Yorker—who persistently ignored the farm etiquette of maintaining his section of line fences. Not only did the neighbor neglect the fences, but he seemed to have a way of enlarging small openings until his cattle could get through to feed on another man's grass. Pleas, then protest, repeated again and again, seemed not to move the Yorker, who, incidentally, made a good deal of money by selling what he claimed to be pedigreed black-and-white "Dutch Belt" cattle. A red Jersey bull, staked out inconspicuously in the field so frequently invaded by the black-and-white cows, effected a cure of the fence-neglecting neighbor. When, nine months after the bull had been in the field, calves with red markings began to appear in the neighbor's herd, there was no possibility for him to claim the pure pedigree. Thus was the matter of a disputed property fence settled without further protest or argument.

Poor Judge

Sometime during the early half of the nineteenth century, there lived in Poultney one William Ward, who served twenty years as justice of the peace, then as judge of the probate court.

> John Tilden, a somewhat eccentric and cunning sort of man, made application to the town . . . for an abatement

of his taxes on account of poverty. Judge Ward said Tilden was as able to pay taxes as he was.

Tilden turned to him and said, "Judge Ward, you don't know anything about poverty, you never was poor!"

His answer, "Yes, I was."

Tilden says, "Was you ever so poor that you have lived months together without pork in your house and at times without bread, and for years had hard work to get enough provisions to keep your family from starving? Was you ever so poor that you was obliged to send your children to bed crying for supper, and you had none to give them?"

Ward answered again, "Yes, I have been."

"Well," says Tilden, "I must confess I never was so poor as that," and sat down satisfied and pursued his petition no further.

Further comment from the writer adds, "Very few of the inhabitants could in truth have answered the same questions in a different way. Samuel Church and family lived one season almost entirely on ground nuts. The writer of this lived two seasons when a boy almost as bad off."

Poor Deacon

All across early Vermont poverty was so much a way of life that a man with even a little more than his neighbor expected to lend a helping hand. In this respect Captain Trotter of Bradford was known to be particularly generous. One town meeting day there came to him elderly Deacon Ford who, having lost his only cow, could not see how he and his wife were to survive. Would not, he begged, the Captain start a subscription to help him purchase another cow? Captain Trotter, knowing the man's circumstances, promptly agreed. He wrote the following lines which he read out to his townfolk when assembled for the town meeting:

"Charity never knocked louder than now.
A poor old couple have lost their cow!
The cow belonged to Deacon Ford—
Give to the poor and lend to the Lord."

To this, Captain Trotter signed his name, also noting the liberal sum he was subscribing, then passed the paper around. To the great joy of the poor Deacon, enough was shortly subscribed not only to buy another cow but to supply it with hay for months ahead.

Captain Morey's Invention

Samuel Morey, born in Connecticut in 1762, arrived in Orford (then considered a part of Vermont but today in New Hampshire) on the Connecticut River. He was four years old and sometime later moved across the river to Fairlee, Vermont. With a talent for mechanics and engineering, the future Captain Morey would eventually be put in charge of the construction and operation of the river locks at Bellows Falls, those locks through which moved the river traffic from Hartford, Connecticut, on up the river as far as settlements reached.

As early as 1790 Captain Morey was experimenting with ways for applying steam power to the saving of labor. Among these were a steam-operated spit, which he patented, and a steam engine which, when set in the bow of a small craft, could propel it. This he demonstrated on the river.

Like scientists of today, obsessed with ways to harness energy for man's benefit, Morey continued to patent a variety of then-novel devices. Before 1800, he had patented a rotary steam engine, a windmill, a waterwheel, and a steam pump. Later, in 1826, he obtained one of the first American patents for an internal combustion engine. From the *Boston Recorder* comes a quote:

> Capt. Samuel Morey, as early as 1791 or 1792, applied steam power to a small boat on the Connecticut River at this place (Fairlee) and afterwards on Fairlee Pond now renamed Lake Morey in his honor which worked with admirable success, considering the infancy and consequent imperfection of the invention, or the application of steam power to navigation.

In 1797, Morey demonstrated on the Delaware River the feasibility of powering river boats with steam engines. Having failed to persuade one viewer, Robert Fulton, to support his further efforts, Morey always felt Fulton appropriated his own ideas. History, however, has seen many similar nearly contemporaneous inventions coming from demonstrably separate sources. When the time is ripe for an invention, inventive minds like Morey's become aware both of the need and of the possibility of supplying it. In any case, Morey was not the one to win the fame or the backing for steam-powered boats.

The Village Blacksmith

Like other forms of the creative urge, the inventive urge has a way of possessing itself of the most unexpected people. Such was blacksmith Davenport of Brandon. Orphaned Thomas Davenport, whose formal schooling was limited to a total of three years, was apprenticed in 1816, at the age of fourteen, to a blacksmith in Williamstown, Vermont. In 1823, having reached his majority, Davenport's apprenticeship ended and he moved to Brandon, where his elder brother, Barzilla, was already a practicing attorney.

To a blacksmith shop, such as Tom established in Brandon, came the men of the town with orders for ironware, with horses and oxen to be shod, and with the day's latest gossip. Thus, in 1833 the young blacksmith's ears heard talk of an amazing electromagnet used at the Pennfield Iron Works across Lake Champlain at Crown Point, New York. Accounts of what this new device was able to do in the way of lifting iron so stirred Tom's imagination that he became determined to witness the wonder with his own eyes. Somehow, without funds to pay for ferry or stagecoach transportation, he made his way to Crown Point, but to his disappointment, "the proprietors were not at home" and the magnet therefore could not be viewed.

Still haunted by the magnet and no less determined than ever to see it, Tom persuaded his brother Oliver to help him. Oliver was a tin peddler and clock tinker who drove his cart—a combination hardware shop—around the countryside from house to house, selling his wares and his skills. Sixty years later, when Oliver had reached the age of ninety, he would recall with brotherly pride his long-dead brother's obsession. With most of the rest of his world, however, he had no real understanding of the amazing achievement of his self-taught blacksmith brother.

"I was peddling," he reminisced, "when Tom sent me word to come to Brandon and go with him to Crown Point to buy the magnet. I went to Brandon and Tom and I started for Crown Point in my peddler's wagon. It was toward the spring of the year, and when we got to Charlotte, there was a big crack in the ice of the creek, and I said, 'We cannot get over it and must go back.' Tom said, 'No, we cannot go back; jump the horse over,' and I did, and we went to Crown Point, reaching there Saturday night. There we saw the magnet. It was shaped like a horse shoe, the arms ten or twelve inches long, and spreading six inches, and wound with wire back and forth, perhaps an inch thick."

Tom Davenport's reaction was more exalted than his down-to-earth brother's. "Here to me was one of the wonders of Nature and of Providence!" he wrote later. "Like a flash of lightning the thought occurred to me that here was an available power which was within the reach of man. If three pounds of iron and copper wire would suspend in the air 150 pounds, what would three hundred pounds suspend? 'In a few years,' I said to some gentlemen present, 'steamboats will be propelled by this power.' A by-stander said to me, 'You mean, sir, magnetic boats?' 'Truly so,' I remarked, 'and ere long this mysterious power will supercede steam, for shall this mighty agent which suspends between heaven and earth this mass of iron serve no other purpose than to excite our wonder and admiration?'"

Those were years when explosions of steam boilers were frequent and often fatal; so Tom Davenport's dream of replacing the "murderous power of steam" with electricity was for the welfare of mankind in general rather than for his personal profit. Actually, in securing a magnet, he immediately incurred an indebtedness from which he was to free himself only with the greatest difficutly.

"The price of the little thing was $75.00!" his shocked brother recalled. "This was more than we had and I tried to persuade Tom to leave it, but he said 'No,' he must have the magnet, and he proposed that I should sell goods from my peddler's cart and raise the money. So I went ahead with the auction . . . It was soon evident that no $75.00 could be got out of the auction, but that Tom was not going back without his magnet. And so, while I was busy auctioneering, he swapped my horse for a poor beast, so old that I could eat more hay than she could, and by putting in the boot of the horse trade with the proceeds of the auction, and scraping together all the money we both had in our pockets, we got the magnet, Tom promising to see me whole again, which he did. I was sick enough of the whole business, though, at the time, and told Tom we shouldn't have enough money to buy a dinner on the way home, and he said, 'Never mind, maybe we shan't want any,' and he was happy with his magnet."

Oliver immediately began to think of ways to earn back the great sum they had spent in Crown Point. Undoubtedly he didn't relish being seen around the countryside with the disreputable nag Tom had gotten for him in exchange for his horse. Why not, he suggested, exhibit the magnet and charge a fee for the demonstration? Everybody who'd heard about it was dying to see it and they'd go home and talk to others and soon people would flock from far away. Maybe, after all, the magnet could earn them a profit!

Again Tom said, "No!" He had not bought the magnet to exhibit it but to study it, to find out how it was put together so that, having learned its secrets, he could make a magnet for himself and, perhaps, bring to eventual realization his dream of "magnetic boats."

Of course Oliver protested and of course in vain. "I begged him not to destroy the magnet," he told the interviewer, "but he was determined and said he could make another, and the first thing he did that night, he and Emily, his wife, set down, she with pen, ink, and paper, he with the magnet, and he commenced to unwind the wire. She had a fine education, and was as enthusiastic as he was, and wrote down exactly the way the wire was wound on, and all about it. The next thing he did was to go to his blacksmith's shop and make another 'horse shoe' of soft iron many times larger than the first. Then he and Emily wound it. First a coating of glue was put on the iron, then it had to be wound with silk, and Emily tore up her silk wedding gown into strips, and used that, and the coils of the wire had to be wound on without touching, or else the whole thing would be spoiled, and then went through and finished it, with silk between each layer of wire; and the magnet was a grand one, and it would lift 'a ton a minute.'"

What a sight it must have been—those two heads bent close in the doubtful light of costly candles or, perhaps, whale oil lamps, while neighbors, seeing the light burning far into the night, made shocked comments on Tom's extravagance.

Though Emily had had more formal education than her husband, neither of them could have known anything about the force they were trying to recreate. Few of the stilted textbooks available in the 1830s troubled to mention anything as elusive and unimportant as electricity. One *Dictionary of Philosophical Terms* defined it as "an invisible, subtle fluid that appears to pervade all nature." Invisible, subtle, and fluid—this was what Tom and Emily set about to capture and make do their bidding. Were ever two innocents setting themselves more impossible a goal!

"Tom kept right on working and working and studying," Oliver remembered. "His idea was to make a wheel revolve by the force of

magnetism, and he seemed possessed of the idea that some day machinery, steamboats, and railroad cars would be run that way."

"In July, 1834," Tom himself wrote, "I succeeded in moving a wheel about seven inches in diameter at the rate of about thirty revolutions a minute. It had four electromagnets, two of which were on the wheel, and two were stationary and placed near the periphery of the revolving wheel."

Here was the first direct-current motor of a type later commonly used for trolley cars. Unfortunately, it could not be used profitably until someone found a better source of electric power than the battery cups available in Tom Davenport's day.

Davenport's neighbors started the rumor that he would soon exhibit a wonderful perpetual motion machine which would astonish everybody. Tom, feeling that such a ridiculous rumor belittled him and made his engine no better than some kind of sideshow trickery, angrily "denied the disgraceful assertion of having any faith in the ingenuity of man to ever accomplish what science and philosophy pronounced impossible."

It was not science and philosophy but the unsophisticated minds of fellow-townsmen he had to deal with. To them any motive power other than that of the familiar waterwheels would seem neither more nor less impossible than perpetual motion. Inevitably, the exhibition Tom arranged to enlighten them was bound to fail.

"I exhibited the wonderful power of my magnet," Tom wrote, "and explained its object, which was to apply it as a new motive power, which would no doubt eventually supercede steam. But this notion did not 'take': there were more believers in perpetual motion than in magnetic power, and my credit would have stood higher if I had allowed the report to go that I was after perpetual motion."

Like any man treading the lonely paths of discovery, Tom still yearned for understanding. Surely, he thought, the parson, with his fine education, could understand and would give him encouragement if he explained his machine and the wonderful benefits he knew it would bring to all mankind.

The parson, it turned out, was a man who did not believe in interfering with the scheme of things as he knew God had arranged them. "Now, Tom," he rebuked his visitor not too unkindly, "if this wonderful power was good for anything it would have been in use long before this."

Seventeen years later, in 1851, the year of his death, Tom recalled the dreams and the bitterness that first engine of his represented. "The power," he wrote, "was sufficient to raise a few ounces one foot high per minute, yet I found the cost per diem of using it on a large scale would be enormous. But I reasoned there would be much improvement in the expense of galvanism as there formerly had been in steam. And it has been so . . . For myself I was satisfied with my labor for the past year, and flattered myself that I should no longer suffer the ridicule and derision of my neighbors and friends, but it was not so. The report spread like wildfire that the 'perpetual motion man' had succeeded in producing a 'mosquito power.'"

Finally Tom turned for understanding to those who knew something about science and its laws. One bleak December day, he packed up his machine and mustered his courage to walk the twenty cold miles to Middlebury College. As he hesitated on the college steps, he "saw a fellow, in a very ragged coat and an old rusty cap turned over his ears . . . and a large dirty plank on his shoulder, about entering the college door with myself. I accosted him and inquired if I should be likely to find Professor Turner about there. He said, 'Yes; come in, and I will show him to you.' I walked into the lumber room; the fellow threw the plank down, pulled off his leather mittens and said, 'I am Professor Turner. You see, I don't look much like a Professor.'"

With instinctive diplomacy, Davenport replied, "As to that, sir, I could not say, for you are the first professor I ever saw and I conclude that your judgment does not lie in your clothes."

The professor liked this outspoken, self-taught young man, liked his enthusiasm and sense of dedication, and approved of his work. Turner called in another professor and together they discussed the machine, both appearing convinced that it would prove "one of the greatest inventions of the nineteenth century" and that it should be patented at once. Tom, apparently, had not thought of that but they soon convinced him, wrote letters of recommendation, and offered assistance in making out a patent application.

Somehow Tom managed to scrape together enough money to send a model of his machine, together with the patent application, to Washington—just in time to be destroyed by a fire which gutted the Patent Office. So he had to start over again, this time going to Washington himself. He filed the application and, on February 25, 1837, received the coveted patent.

Thomas Davenport needed more than a patent; he needed money and something else that men did not yet seem to be fully aware of. However, no generous man held out an encouraging and helpful hand, while unscrupulous promoters used the glowing tributes to Tom's work made by Professor Turner and Professor Silliman of Yale, as well as the *New York Herald,* for their own advancement. They kept the no-longer-young Vermont inventor working on, with empty promises, until both his resources and his strength were exhausted.

In the end, he admitted sadly, "After struggling along . . . trying to convince my friends that the object of which I had so long been in pursuit was still worthy of their attention, I reluctantly gave up hope of further assistance and, in the fall of 1842, moved my family to Brandon, Vermont, where I resumed my trade as a blacksmith, which was then my only resource to gain a livelihood."

Thus, at the age of forty, after years of work and of wandering, trying to find partners, trying to interest investors but only interesting those with no money to invest, Thomas Davenport bitterly swallowed his pride and returned to the town he had left in high hopes and to his "only resource to gain a livelihood."

The failure was not really due to Davenport's so limited educational background nor to the basic impracticability of his invention, which was later used in a somewhat revised form to run trolley cars. His real problem—though neither he nor the learned professors recognized it—was that it came too soon. The important missing link in the chain of invention would, for nearly a quarter of a century, remain missing. Needed was a dynamo which could produce a steady, strong flow of power. Thomas Davenport had had to power his invention with batteries, but batteries would never do to run those steamboats he dreamed of the first time he was vouchsafed a look at an electromagnet.

It was the seemingly stony unwillingness of most people to understand what he was trying to do that hurt Tom most. There was nothing personal in this, for public acceptance of a radically new invention demands new ways of looking at or doing old things. For most people it is much harder to visualize the ways and value of something unfamiliar than to keep on plodding in old ruts. Public response to the first magnetic telegraph in Poultney illustrates this all too well.

Messages Along the Wires

It was told of the first "Magnetic Telegraph" line which was erected in Poultney in 1848:

> Soon after the line was put in working order, he (the operator) received a message from the western part of New York for a well-to-do farmer living a mile or two from the village. The message was enclosed in an envelope and delivered as directed, soon after which the farmer entered the office building holding the message in his hand and, with a peculiar expression of countenance, enquired, "I want you should tell me how you got this letter so quick."
>
> "It come by telegraph."
>
> "What! Do you pretend this letter came three hundred miles by telegraph today?"—holding up the same—"See, it's hardly wrinkled at all! I should like to know how it got

Vermonters—Usual and Unusual

181

through them glass knobs on the poles. I should suppose it would have been all tore to pieces."

A year later, the ways of a telegraph still puzzled townspeople. When President Zachary Taylor's inaugural message was received over the wire, it was immediately written down by someone who sat by as the operator dictated it. Recorded by 2:00 P.M. on town meeting day, it was delivered to a deacon who read it to the assembled crowd. People insisted it must be a fake—that the operator had copied some old document and was imposing it on them as the president's words. "But when the papers were received from New York the next day, and the same article read, unbelief gave way to faith." Suddenly people must have begun to expect of the telegraph achievements as impossible as the perpetual motion expected of poor Thomas Davenport.

Potatomania

Agriculturally minded folk who failed to understand scientific inventions seemed to have had no trouble at all in grasping the importance of new horticultural varieties. Bigger, better, tastier fruits and vegetables—these immediately took hold of the imaginations of folk who just couldn't believe that telegrams could survive untorn their journey along the wires.

One notable breeder of plants was Cyrus Guernsey Pringle of Charlotte, Vermont. In 1873 he wrote to a Boston correspondent:

> May I introduce myself as a young farmer, hardly a farmer by choice for my college studies were terminated abruptly by the death of a brother, our mother's chief dependence on the farm, and our circumstances seemed to render it imperative that I should take his place. My taste has led me to give my farming a decidedly horticultural character . . .

In another letter he wrote:

> Hybridization is a subject to which I have assiduously devoted myself for several years, reading everything on the subject which I can obtain, whether in French or English, and experimenting so much as I have opportunity upon numerous varieties of plants, fruits, cereals, flowers, etc.

"Beside my usual cares," Pringle wrote later, "I have to grow a large quantity of potatoes of a new variety of my own originating (a cross between Excelsior and Early Rose)." It was a good variety and had Pringle been commercially minded he might have turned his flair for breeding new plants into a profitable business. He, however, was more interested in less specially applied botany and was presently gaining a reputation in that area which would take him on plant-collecting trips to the newly opening Southwest as well as on into Mexico. His collections are still housed at the University of Vermont in the Pringle Herbarium.

Other Vermonters were already busying themselves with developing new and wonderful kinds of potatoes—a Mr. Ryand, a Mr. Alexander living not too far from Pringle's Charlotte home, a Rutland farmer, name not given, and Mr. Albert Bresee, of Hubbardton, who claimed to have originated the Early Rose potato, for one seed ball of which the sum of $50 had been offered. The unimpressed historian of Hubbardton gives a delightful account of the business:

> As the fabled palace of Aladdin was incomplete without the roc's egg on the summit of its dome, so would our annals be unfinished without some account of "Early Rose," the last but not least of modern humbugs . . . we may ill forbear to mention how one hill of tubers (the seed of which was purloined from a neighbor's garden) realized to the lucky———something over $700, paying off a mortgage debt—one person taking eight potatoes, giving $400 cash but cutting his seed so fine it never grew. How another giving $25 for a tuber which might have been encircled by a lady's ring; holding the entire product in his hand a year after, bestowed them on his hog, giving them as they went an Indian curse; how one half bushel derived from some uncertain source, realized, as rumor goes, to the possessor about $1800.
>
> How Mr. A in his peregrination over the country found a couple of tubers of some unknown variety, the product of which (one peck) some were willing to accept as No. 4 of Bresee's in their eagerness to secure that secret to wealth. The miller agreeing to furnish him with flour and give him $5 in money for one, the blacksmith agreeing to shoe his horse for three years for another.

"So nicely humbugged folks did get," concludes the once-popular ballad which was set to music and sung at a festival. It runs thus:

> There was a man I once did know,
> And he was wondrous wise,
> He raised potatoes very fine,

And dug out all their eyes;
And these he sold for piles of gold,
For so the story goes,
He gave a blessing on them all,
And called them "Early Rose."
And such a time as men did have
To watch them night and day,
I vow, before I'd have such work
I'd throw myself away

. . . .
So men, they travelled day and night
Without regard to health
To beg or borrow, buy or steal,
This source of princely wealth,
And very lucky was that chap
For so the story goes,
Who in his travels could obtain
A peck of "Early Rose."

. . . .
One man, by witchcraft yet unknown,
Obtained a number four,
And when men asked to see the sight,
He pointed to the door.
I feared his reason nigh had fled
So wildly glared his eyes;
No miser ever watched his gold
With vigilance more wise.

Presently, "deacons, doctors, priests and all" were caught by the mania until someone finally diagnosed it as "potatoes on the brain."

This potatomania sounds as if closely related to the tulip mania that raged throughout the seventeenth-century Netherlands. It was, a historian tells, "so great that the ordinary industry of the country was neglected . . . until, in the year 1635, many persons were known to invest a fortune of 100,000 florins (possibly the equivalent of $45,000 today) for the purchase of forty roots" of some new kind of tulip.

All of this suggests that people, whatever their land or era, whether born in seventeenth-century Holland or nineteenth-century Vermont, do not differ in any very fundamental way. Whatever their origins, people are, by and large, equally knowledgeable, equally foolish—always interesting, always baffling, always worth learning about so that we may understand one another better.

Postscript:

A Unique Vermonter

Anyone who has read part of this book may have begun wondering how so very many vivid reminiscences of early Vermont folk and their ways could be available so long after the incidents described and the anecdotes recounted should have joined the ranks of forgotten bits of history. Battles and generals and politicians are too often remembered while the people for and by whom the battles were fought and by whom the politicians were voted into power are lost in the dim mists of the past. Year by year memory fades, and unless a special effort is made to revive it, understanding is lost beyond recall.

Fearing just this kind of oblivion for her beloved state and perceiving the urgency of doing something about it if ever anything was to be done, a very special Vermonter named Abby Maria Hemenway undertook a century ago, without outside support and with little encouragement, to preserve the history of her state with the kind of personal detail that makes history come alive.

She was a remarkable woman, Abby Maria, born in Ludlow in 1828 of a family that had settled there in 1790. Her father recalled when there was but one house in town. An intelligent, gifted girl, she began teaching district school in Ludlow when only fourteen years old. Four years later she had enrolled herself in Ludlow's Black River Academy. From the Academy she was to progress to a teaching

185

post in neighboring Mt. Holly, undertaking all three terms—summer, fall, winter—and boarding around according to standard custom. There she experienced everything from a two-week stint of dandelion greens three times a day to the more delightful and apparently more frequent kind of home, a description of whose meals can even now make the mouth water.

When Abby was offered a teaching post at a local Select School, she readily accepted it, later recording the feeling comment:

> They that know nothing fear nothing. I took the school, nothing doubting. I had sixteen scholars old enough to go into company with me . . . It required some tact to rule in a school-room all those young, daring, inglorious spirits . . . It was a hard spot.

Hard spots never made her wince. Soon she followed the example of many another Vermont schoolmarm and went west to teach. After six not-too-happy years in Michigan, she returned home in 1858 and published a collection of poems by Vermonters. Through this effort, she caught the wider vision of filling the gaps in Vermont history by means of a gazetteer which was to collect histories and personal reminiscences, county by county and town by town, until there was fixed for posterity the kinds of accounts only to be made available while the men and women who participated in them still lived in fact or in the memories of their own children.

With practically no encouragement and no financial backing at all, Abby Maria faced the task she set herself and never, for the thirty-odd remaining years of her life, relinquished her dream. She traveled the rough roads from town to town, enlisting willing contributors, somehow persuading the reluctant. To support her efforts she issued quarterly copies of her *Gazetteer* as it progressed, selling each issue for twenty-five cents a copy. The accumulated dollars were to pay for typesetting, paper, and printing of the next issue. Starting with Addison County, she intended to follow through the counties in alphabetical order. Windsor, her own county, was never printed.

Dedicated, single-minded, increasingly eccentric as the lean years passed, she ran up debts until, to compensate themselves, her creditors confiscated Volume IV. Yet it was only by selling this volume that she could hope to get on with the next. Without qualms of conscience, one night she invaded the bindery where those books were stored and took them, soon moving them on to Chicago, beyond easy reach of her clamoring Vermont creditors. In Chicago, she continued her work, living a recluse's life, setting the type for Volume V by herself. There, alone in a shabby rooming house, she died of apoplexy in February, 1890, leaving behind the uncompleted Volume V for her sister in Vermont to see through press. The trunk containing manuscript material for Volume VI was seized by Chicago creditors and eventually lost when the house where it had been stored burned down.

A comparison of the later-published comparatively dull Windsor County history with Abby Maria Hemenway's kind of records illustrates how valuable were the volumes produced by that unique Vermonter. Ironically, some thirty years after her death, the state of Vermont, which during her life had contributed no more than a grudging $500 to her efforts, had become so aware of the value of her work as to allot $12,000 to the task of having her five volumes, totaling more than 6,000 pages, indexed. Even a quarter of that sum, had it been expended forty years earlier, could have eased Abby Maria Hemenway's burden of debt and made it possible for her to spend her last years among friends in the Vermont she so loved.

With deep appreciation this writer admits her indebtedness to the Vermont historian, Abby Maria Hemenway. Her *Vermont Historical Gazetteer* was published as follows: Vol. I, 1867; Vol. II, 1871; Vol. III, 1877; Vol. IV, 1882; Vol. V, 1891. Her efforts, we suspect, may have contributed to the flowering of town histories which took place a century ago at about the time of town and state centennial celebrations. Many of the contributors to the *Gazetteer* were also authors of those sometimes exceedingly interesting volumes, with occasional detail not included in the shorter accounts published in the *Gazetteer*. Of those town histories, the following have been especially interesting to this writer: Brandon, Danby, Middletown, Pawlet, Pittsford, Poultney, and Salisbury. Many are quoted herein.

Anyone wishing to read further or desiring to locate other quotes in their original settings might find some of them in Hager's *Geology of Vermont* (1861), in Hall's *History of Eastern Vermont* (1858), Rowland Robinson's *Vermont: A Study of Independence* (1892), Siebert's *The Underground Railroad* (1898) and, of course, Ethan Allen's own *Narrative,* reissued in the American Experience Series by Corinth Books. An interesting biography of Ethan Allen by Charles A. Jellison was issued some years ago by the Syracuse University Press (see the list of sources, which follows). Parts of it make fascinating reading but it is not quoted here.

All of these books mentioned, except the reissued Ethan Allen *Narrative,* are rare and on gradually disintegrating paper. You will find that most libraries hoard them on locked shelves.

The author found the following books and printed materials of assistance in the writing of this book. The list includes both books read for general background and those quoted in the text. Whenever a particular wcrk has furnished source material for a particular chapter or chapters of this book, the chapter(s) involved appear in parentheses after the entry. When an entry is not followed by any chapter number, the work in question is of general interest.

Aldrich, Lewis C., and Holmes, Frank R. (eds.). *History of Windsor County.* Syracuse, N.Y.: D. Mason & Co., 1891. (Chapter 6)

Allen, Ethan. *A Narrative of Colonel Ethan Allen's Observations During His Captivity.* 1779. Reprint, New York: Corinth Books, 1930. (Chapter 2)

Campbell, Tom W. *The Fighters and Two Fines: Sketches of the Lives of Matthew Lyon and Andrew Jackson.* Little Rock, Ark.: Pioneer Publishing Co., 1941. (Chapter 2)

Caverly, A. M. *History of the Town of Pittsford, Vt.* Rutland, Vt.: Tuttle & Co., 1872. (Chapters 1 and 2)

Davenport, Walter Rice. *Thomas Davenport, Pioneer Inventor.* Montpelier: Vermont Historical Society, 1929. (Chapter 12)

Dodge, Bertha S. *Engineering Is Like This.* Boston: Little, Brown, 1963. (Chapter 12)

———. *Potatoes and People.* Boston: Little, Brown, 1970. (Chapter 10)

Fisher, Dorothy Canfield. *Vermont Tradition: The Biography of an Outlook on Life.* Boston: Little, Brown, 1953.

Frisbie, Barnes. *History of Middletown.* Rutland, Vt.: Tuttle & Co., 1867. (Chapter 9)

Greeley, Horace, et al. *The Great Industries of the United States.* Hartford, Conn.: Burr & Hyde, 1872. (Chapter 7)

Hager, Albert D. "Economical Geology of Vermont." In *Geology of Vermont,* vol. 2, part 9, pp. 773-870. Claremont, N.H.: Claremont Manufacturing Co., 1861. (Chapters 7 and 9)

Hall, Benjamin H. *History of Eastern Vermont.* New York: D. Appleton & Co., 1858. (Chapters 5, 9, and 11)

Hemenway, Abby Maria (ed.). *Vermont Historical Gazetteer.* 1 (1867), 2 (1871), 3 (1877), 4 (1882), 5 (1891).

Hollister, Hiel. *Pawlet for One Hundred Years.* Albany: J. Munsell, 1867. (Chapters 4, 5, 7, and 10)

Jellison, Charles A. *Ethan Allen, Frontier Rebel.* Syracuse, N.Y.: Syracuse University Press, 1969.

Joslin, Joseph, et al. *History of Town of Poultney.* Poultney, Vt.: Journal Printing Office, 1875. (Chapters 5 and 6)

Morrissey, Brenda C. (ed.). *Abby Hemenway's Vermont.* Brattleboro, Vt.: Stephen Greene Press, 1972.

Pell, John. *Ethan Allen.* Boston: Houghton Mifflin Co., 1929.

Robinson, Rowland E. *Vermont: A Study of Independence.* Boston: Houghton Mifflin Co., 1892. (Chapter 9)

Saxe, John Godfrey. *Poems.* Boston: Houghton Mifflin Co., 1873. (Chapter 7)

Siebert, Wilbur H. *The Underground Railroad from Slavery to Freedom.* New York: Macmillan Co., 1898. (Chapter 9)

Thompson, Charles Miner. *Independent Vermont.* Boston: Houghton Mifflin Co., 1942.

Weeks, John W. *History of Salisbury, Vermont.* Middlebury, Conn.: A. H. Copeland, 1860. (Chapters 2, 9, 11, and 12)

Williams, J. C. *History and Map of Danby, Vermont.* Rutland, Vt.: McLean & Robbins, 1869. (Chapters 6, 9, and 11)

Williams, Samuel. *The Natural and Civil History of Vermont.* 2 vols. Burlington, Vt.: 1809.

Index